Copyright © 2025

All rights reserved. No part of this publication may be reproduced, distributed, or transmitted in any form or by any means without the prior written permission of the author. All Wikimedia images are in the public domain.

Dedication

This Book is dedicated to
the Lord Jesus Christ.

Acknowledgements

My humble gratitude for the inspiration of the Holy Spirit
who guided this work.
To my wonderful wife, Telli, whose love and support helped me finish this
project through many health concerns.
To those who encouraged me.
To Pastor Charlie, whose passion for the Word of God, in-depth study of the
original Greek, and comprehensive commentaries ensured the theological
soundness of this work, despite his own health concerns, pastoral duties,
and struggles with hurricanes and Chihuahuas.
To all the gifted artists, past and present, whose inclusion in this work help us
connect to the individuals and events recorded in Scripture.

Forward

This New Testament pictorial book will be a game-changer for your understanding of Scripture. It pairs key passages from the New Testament with stunning historical paintings that bring the events to life. Each page feels like stepping into a moment—whether it's the Nativity, the Sermon on the Mount, or the Crucifixion—illustrated by masterful artworks from centuries past. The text is clear and concise, explaining the context and meaning of each passage, while the paintings add a vivid, emotional depth that makes the stories feel immediate and real. It's a beautiful blend of faith, history, and art that will surely deepen your connection to the precious Word of God.

Emlen S. "Charlie" Garrett
Pastor, The Superior Word
Sarasota, Florida

Forgiven

Christ and the Sinner by Andrey Mironov (2011)

Preface

The Volume of the Book: Christ in the Old Testament was written to show how prophecy predicted the Son of God's mission, how many events foreshadowed His sacrifice, and how He took the form of the Angel of the Lord to physically shape events.

The Volume of the Book: Christ in the New Testament was written to show how prophecy was fulfilled through the Son of God's love, compassion, and tenacity in facing the trials and threats of opposing individuals. It reveals how He engaged the people who eventually believed in His divinity. It also details interactions with those who assisted Him in spreading the message that His death was intended to break them free from law and sin. Through this, they could be filled with God's Spirit, shaping their lives to become one with God.

This life is about finding God (Acts 17:26-27). The Bible tells His story. Choose wisely. May the grace of the Lord be with you.

Warning—*we wrestle not against flesh and blood, but against the rulers, against the authorities, against the cosmic powers over this present darkness, against the spiritual forces of evil in the heavenly places.* (Ephesians 6:12)

Cover: The Risen Christ appearing to the Virgin by Jacques Stella (1640)

Scripture in Italics – guided by the English Standard Version

Table of Contents

The Beginning	2	Lazarus	50
Angelic Visits	4	Power Flows	52
Presentation at the Temple	6	Lord of the Sabbath	54
Earthly Father and Son	8	Challenge of the Pharisees	56
At Twelve	10	Doing Good	58
Carpenters	12	Woe to You	60
The Baptism	14	Hypocrisy	62
The Wilderness	16	The Sower	64
Wild Animals and Angels	18	Pearl of Great Price	66
Gathering Disciples	20	Miracles	68
Cana	22	Dealing with Demons	70
Blasphemy at the Temple	24	Control over Nature	72
Jesus' Fame Spreads	26	Transfiguration	74
Nicodemus	28	Let the Little Ones Come	76
Samaritan Woman	30	Tribute Money	78
Sermon on the Mount	32	Weeps over Jerusalem	80
Beatitudes	34	Last Supper	82
Perfection	36	Jesus' Prayer	84
Narrow Road	38	Agony in Gethsemane	86
Sermon Continues	40	The Sword	88
His Authority	42	On Trial	90
Healing	44	Sanhedrin	92
Widow of Nain's Son	46	King Herod	94
Raising the Dead	48	Righteous Man	96

Crucifixion	98
God is Love	100
Sepulcher	102
Sheol	104
Rising from the Dead	106
Enthusiasm	108
Examine Me	110
Reconciliation	112
Great Commission	114
Pentecost	116
Peter Preaching	118
The Ethiopian	120
Conversion of Saul	122
Filled with the Spirit	124
Tabitha	126
Cornelius	128
Disagreements	130
False Prophets	132
Athens	134
Eutychus	136
Trial	138
Shipwreck	140
Malta	142
Brother of Jesus - James	144
Another Brother – Jude	146
Leader's Guidance	148
Apostle – Paul	150
Love - Paul	152
Doctrine - Paul	154
Endtime Events - Paul	156
Armor of God	158
Spreading the Word	160
Beloved Apostle	162
Patmos – Revelation	164
Last Judgment	166
Dispensations	168
Aftermath	170
Humble Beginnings	172
Just Ask	174
Witness	176
Rejoice in Suffering	178
Peace and Security	180
Why?	182
The Chosen	184
Illustrations and Art	186
Editor	191

Christ in the New Testament

In the Beginning
John 1

God Creating by Jan Brueghel the Younger (17th century)

In the beginning was the Word, and the Word was God... All things were made through Him... the Word became flesh and dwelt among us... to all who received Him, He gave the right to become children of God... grace and truth came through Jesus Christ.

Grace is unmerited favor. You simply have to believe and accept.

Isn't this our hope? To become a child of God?

John's gospel emphasizes Christ as the Son of God, and His life as divine intervention in the world for the purpose of redeeming His creation. Through His work, man is promised to be provided an eternal, joyful, and productive existence.

God provides the written Word to explain how and where creation veered off path and to show the way back to harmony with Him. Because we are unable to accomplish the task on our own, our Creator chose to take on human form and pay the penalty for the error of mankind. This unfathomable, deep love is breathtaking. It should drive us to our knees in humility, thankfulness, and love.

New Testament books are eyewitness accounts of Jesus Christ's divinity and explain His prophetic presence, intention, and actions. Read them seriously.

Annunciation
Luke 1

The Dream
Matthew 1

The Annunciation of the Virgin
by Gregorio Martínez (1547-1598)

The Dream of Saint Joseph
by Philippe de Champaigne (1642-1643)

Both Mary and Joseph knew they were to protect, nurture, and raise God's Son.

The angel Gabriel was sent from God to a city of Galilee named Nazareth, to a virgin betrothed to a man whose name was Joseph, of the house of David. And the virgin's name was Mary. And the angel said to her, "Do not be afraid, Mary, for you have found favor with God. And behold, you will conceive in your womb and bear a Son, and you shall call His name Jesus. He will be great and will be called the Son of the Most High. And the Lord God will give to Him the throne of His father David, and He will reign over the house of Jacob forever, and of His kingdom there will be no end."

When His mother Mary had been betrothed to Joseph, before they came together, she was found to be with Child from the Holy Spirit. And her husband, Joseph, being a just man and unwilling to put her to shame, resolved to divorce her quietly. But as he considered these things, behold, an angel of the Lord appeared to him in a dream, saying, "Joseph, son of David, do not fear to take Mary as your wife, for that which is conceived in her is from the Holy Spirit. She will bear a Son, and you shall call His name Jesus, for He will save His people from their sins."

Luke was a Gentile. His gospel highlights Jesus' humanity and His compassion for the poor and marginalized, while Matthew approaches his gospel from a Levitical perspective, emphasizing Jesus' Old Testament fulfillment.

Presentation at the Temple
Luke 2

Presentation of Jesus at the Temple by Jean André (1662-1753)

Jesus was born in Bethlehem. Eight days later…

…when the time came for their purification according to the Law of Moses, they brought Him up to Jerusalem to present Him to the Lord. Now there was a man in Jerusalem, whose name was Simeon, and this man was righteous and devout, waiting for the consolation of Israel, and the Holy Spirit was upon him. And it had been revealed to him by the Holy Spirit that he would not see death before he had seen the Lord's Christ. And he came in the Spirit into the temple, and when the parents brought in the Child Jesus, to do for Him according to the custom of the Law, he took Him up in his arms and blessed God and said,

"Lord, now You are letting your servant depart in peace, according to Your word; for my eyes have seen Your salvation that You have prepared in the presence of all peoples, a light for revelation to the Gentiles, and for glory to Your people Israel."

And His father and His mother marveled at what was said about Him. And Simeon blessed them and said to Mary His mother, "Behold, this Child is appointed for the fall and rising of many in Israel, and for a sign that is opposed (and a sword will pierce through your own soul also), so that thoughts from many hearts may be revealed."

What does our heart reveal?

Earthly Father and Son
Matthew 2/Mark 6

Saint Joseph and the Christ Child by Guido Reni (1640)

No doubt, Joseph was a loving father, nurturing his adopted Son while living in Bethlehem, where the wise men visited. Their gifts of gold, frankincense, and myrrh represent His kingship, priesthood, and death.

He protected Him in their flight to Egypt because of Herod's vendetta and relocated Him to a safe haven in Nazareth.

Eventually, they brought into the world four other sons (James, Joses, Judas, and Simon) and an unknown number of daughters.

What a blessing to welcome new life into the world. May the Lord guide us in their upbringing.

Mark was reportedly Peter's scribe. His gospel views Jesus as a Servant and is the only synoptic gospel without a genealogy.

And yet, here the Seed of the woman (Genesis 3:15), prophesized 4,000 years earlier, enters His world in order to save it. Thank you, Lord!

At Twelve
Luke 2

The Twelve-year-old Jesus in the Temple by Max Liebermann (1879)

Now His parents went to Jerusalem every year at the Feast of the Passover. And when He was twelve years old, they went up according to custom. And when the feast was ended, as they were returning, the boy Jesus stayed behind in Jerusalem. His parents did not know it, but supposing Him to be in the group, they went a day's journey, but then they began to search for Him among their relatives and acquaintances, and when they did not find Him, they returned to Jerusalem, searching for Him. After three days, they found Him in the Temple, sitting among the teachers, listening to them and asking them questions. And all who heard Him were amazed at His understanding and His answers. And when His parents saw Him, they were astonished. And His mother said to Him, "Son, why have You treated us so? Behold, Your father and I have been searching for You in great distress." And He said to them, "Why were you looking for Me? Did you not know that I must be in My Father's house?" And they did not understand the saying that He spoke to them. And He went down with them and came to Nazareth and was submissive to them.

Jesus was aware of His mission from a young age, knowing the purpose of the Temple, and questioning and answering those in authority. He was, apparently, unafraid of being alone, but honored the wishes of His parents, who were a bit perplexed.

Carpenters
Matthew 13/Mark 6

The Youth of Our Lord by John Rogers Herbert (1847)

We do not know much about Jesus' early life, but we do know people in His hometown referred to Him and His father as carpenters (t*ekton* in Greek, also meaning artisan or craftsman).

What a telling profession, a builder, then He becomes the foundation of the church.

The Baptism
Luke 1/3 – Matthew 3

John the Baptist Baptizing Christ by Francesco Trevisani (1723)

John the Baptist's parents were Zechariah, a priest of the division of Abijah, and Elizabeth, a relative of Jesus' mother, Mary. Before either child was born, an angel visited Zechariah while he was on duty, telling him about John.

You will have joy and gladness, and many will rejoice at his birth, for he will be great before the Lord. And he must not drink wine or strong drink, and he will be filled with the Holy Spirit, even from his mother's womb. And he will turn many of the children of Israel to the Lord their God, and he will go before Him in the spirit and power of Elijah, to turn the hearts of the fathers to the children, and the disobedient to the wisdom of the just, to make ready for the Lord a people prepared.

John preached to and baptized the people, telling them the One who followed would baptize with the Holy Spirit and fire.

He baptized Jesus as well, recognizing their roles should be reversed. This marked the beginning of Jesus' ministry.

John would later be beheaded by Herod because he questioned his example.

In the Wilderness
Matthew 4 – Luke 4

Christ in the Wilderness by Ivan Kramskoy (1872)

Then Jesus wandered in the wilderness for 40 days and nights, which is the biblical period of testing.

Satan imagined he could tempt Jesus to worship him, but Jesus was not susceptible and rebuked him.

Christ's three responses to the devil are important. First: *Man shall not live by bread alone, but by every word from the mouth of God.* Second: *You shall not put the Lord your God to the test.* And third: *You shall worship the Lord your God and Him only shall you serve.* Remember them.

Wild Animals and Angels
Mark 1

Christ in the Wilderness by Moretto da Brescia (1515-1520)

And when Satan departed…

He was with the wild animals, and the angels were ministering to Him.

It's invigorating to ponder our path from time to time and listen to the guidance of the Spirit. Jesus was filled with the Spirit, and we can be too when we humble ourselves and submit to Him.

And you can recognize wisdom from the Spirit, because *the wisdom from above is first pure, then peaceable, gentle, open to reason, full of mercy and good fruits, impartial and sincere* (James 3:17).

Calling His Disciples
John 1 – Matthew 10

The Calling of Saints Peter and Andrew by Caravaggio (1602–1604)

Andrew, a disciple of John the Baptist, heard him saying *Behold, the Lamb of God* about Jesus. He reported they had found the Messiah to his brother, Simon, whom Jesus renamed Cephas, an Aramaic meaning Peter, both mean "Rock."

Thus began the gathering of followers who would help Him spread the Word.

Philip and Nathanael followed shortly after.

He added many disciples, but chose only twelve as apostles, meaning "sent ones." They were designated with a special mission to preach the Good News.

The names of the twelve apostles are these: first, Simon, who is called Peter, and Andrew his brother; James the son of Zebedee, and John his brother; Philip and Bartholomew; Thomas and Matthew the tax collector; James the son of Alphaeus, and Thaddaeus; Simon the Zealot, and Judas Iscariot, who betrayed Him.

He told them, *Behold, I am sending you out as sheep in the midst of wolves, so be wise as serpents and innocent as doves.* We might be well advised to heed such caution. The world is a rather hostile place, because the ruler of this world is evil.

Cana
John 2

Marriage at Cana by Andrey Nikolaevich Mironov (2017)

Jesus and His disciples were invited to a wedding in Cana with His mother.

When the wine ran out, the mother of Jesus said to Him, "They have no wine." And Jesus said to her, "Woman, what does this have to do with Me? My hour has not yet come." His mother said to the servants, "Do whatever He tells you."

Now there were six stone water jars there for the Jewish rites of purification, each holding twenty or thirty gallons. Jesus said to the servants, "Fill the jars with water." And they filled them up to the brim. And He said to them, "Now draw some out and take it to the master of the feast." So, they took it. When the master of the feast tasted the water now become wine, and did not know where it came from (though the servants who had drawn the water knew), the master of the feast called the bridegroom and said to him, "Everyone serves the good wine first, and when people have drunk freely, then the poor wine. But you have kept the good wine until now." This, the first of His signs, Jesus did at Cana in Galilee, and manifested His glory. And His disciples believed in Him.

Jesus respected and honored His mother, as we all should, performing the task He was given even though He knew His time for miracles had not yet arrived.

Blasphemy at the Temple
John 2

Jesus Casting Out the Money Changers at the Temple by Carl Bloch (1800s)

The Passover of the Jews was at hand, and Jesus went up to Jerusalem. In the Temple, He found those who were selling oxen and sheep and pigeons, and the money-changers sitting there. And making a whip of cords, He drove them all out of the Temple, with the sheep and oxen. And He poured out the coins of the money-changers and overturned their tables. And He told those who sold the pigeons, "Take these things away; do not make My Father's house a house of trade." His disciples remembered that it was written, "Zeal for Your house will consume Me." (Psalm 69)

So, the Jews said to Him, "What sign do You show us for doing these things?" Jesus answered them, "Destroy this Temple, and in three days I will raise it up." The Jews then said, "It has taken forty-six years to build this Temple, and will You raise it up in three days?" But He was speaking about the Temple of His body. When, therefore, He was raised from the dead, His disciples remembered that He had said this, and they believed the Scripture and the word that Jesus had spoken.

Blasphemy… blasphemy… trying to make money taking advantage of those there to worship?!

Would that we behave properly in the house of God. Please be respectful.

Jesus' Fame Spreads
Matthew 4

Jesus Heals the Blind and Lame on the Mountain by James Tissot (1886-1894)

The word Gospel comes from the English translation of Greek words meaning good news. At the beginning of this story, the good news is the Messiah has arrived, At the end, the good news is He paid the price for your sins. You are forgiven.

And He went throughout all Galilee, teaching in their synagogues and proclaiming the gospel of the kingdom and healing every disease and every affliction among the people. So, His fame spread throughout all Syria, and they brought Him all the sick, those afflicted with various diseases and pains, those oppressed by demons, those having seizures, and paralytics, and He healed them. And great crowds followed Him from Galilee and the Decapolis, and from Jerusalem and Judea, and from beyond the Jordan.

Nicodemus
John 3

Christ and Nicodemus by Fritz von Uhde (1896)

Nicodemus, a leader of the Pharisees, came secretly to Jesus to learn. This was a man who really wanted to understand. Jesus said…

"Truly, truly, I say to you, unless one is born of water and the Spirit, he cannot enter the kingdom of God. That which is born of the flesh is flesh, and that which is born of the Spirit is spirit. Do not marvel that I said to you, 'You must be born again…'"

Nicodemus said to Him, "How can these things be?" Jesus answered him, "Are you the teacher of Israel and yet you do not understand these things? I have told you earthly things and you do not believe, how can you believe if I tell you heavenly things? No one has ascended into heaven except He who descended from heaven, the Son of Man. And as Moses lifted up the serpent in the wilderness, so must the Son of Man be lifted up, that whoever believes in Him may have eternal life.

"For God so loved the world, that He gave his only Son, that whoever believes in Him should not perish but have eternal life. For God did not send His Son into the world to condemn the world, but in order that the world might be saved through Him."

Nicodemus, unlike most of the Pharisees, came to believe in Jesus and defended Him. How arrogant are some people. Be slow to speak and quick to listen. We do not know it all.

The Samaritan Woman
John 4

Christ and the Samaritan Woman by Pierre Antoine Augustin Verlinde (1823)

Like John the Baptist, Jesus' disciples baptized, but when He learned the Pharisees had assessed that He had more followers than John, they left Judea for Galilee and were crossing Samaria when Jesus met a woman of the land. She was drawing water from a well, and He asked for a drink.

The Samaritan woman said to Him, "How is it that You, a Jew, ask for a drink from me, a woman of Samaria?" (For Jews have no dealings with Samaritans.) Jesus answered her, "If you knew the gift of God, and who it is that is saying to you, 'Give Me a drink,' you would have asked Him, and He would have given you living water." The woman said to Him, "Sir, You have nothing to draw water with, and the well is deep. Where do You get that living water? Are You greater than our father Jacob? He gave us the well and drank from it himself, as did his sons and his livestock." Jesus said to her, "Everyone who drinks of this water will be thirsty again, but whoever drinks of the water that I will give him will never be thirsty again. The water that I will give him will become in him a spring of water welling up to eternal life." The woman said to Him, "Sir, give me this water, so that I will not be thirsty or have to come here to draw water."

She perceived He was a prophet and told Him they awaited a Messiah. *Jesus said to her, "I who speak to you am He."*

He remained with the Samaritans for two days, and many believed in Him. How important it is to be open, indeed ready to learn.

Sermon on the Mount
Matthew 5-7

Jesus Christ Teaching on Mountain by Sealino (2023)

Jesus and His disciples traveled broadly and spoke to many groups of people, who believed in Him as the Savior. Miraculously multiplying fish and loaves of bread helped. (Matthew 15) One of the most famous gatherings was the Sermon on the Mount, which included a presentation of the Beatitudes, the Lord's Prayer, and many other important teachings. People flocked to His presence.

He explained, *Do not think that I have come to abolish the Law or the Prophets; I have not come to abolish them but to fulfill them. For truly, I say to you, until heaven and earth pass away, not an iota, not a dot, will pass from the Law until all is accomplished.* A clear statement of the reliability of scripture in its original language.

He made it quite clear that He was the promised Messiah and possessed the authority of God. What He did not explain was that fulfilling prophecy required His death to pay for their sins, though they could have gleaned that from Isaiah 53 and Psalm 22. That role was given to the evangelists who followed, particularly Paul.

Beatitudes
Matthew 5

The Sermon of the Beatitudes by James Tissot (1886-1896)

He taught who were the blessed. Listen to Him.

Seeing the crowds, He went up on the mountain, and when He sat down, His disciples came to Him. And He opened His mouth and taught them, saying:

Blessed are the poor in spirit, for theirs is the kingdom of heaven.
Blessed are those who mourn, for they shall be comforted.
Blessed are the meek, for they shall inherit the earth.
Blessed are those who hunger and thirst for righteousness, for they shall be satisfied.
Blessed are the merciful, for they shall receive mercy.
Blessed are the pure in heart, for they shall see God.
Blessed are the peacemakers, for they shall be called sons of God.
Blessed are those who are persecuted for righteousness' sake, for theirs is the kingdom of heaven.
Blessed are you when others revile you and persecute you and utter all kinds of evil against you falsely on My account. Rejoice and be glad, for your reward is great in heaven, for so they persecuted the prophets who were before you.

Perfection
Matthew 5

Sermon On the Mount by Carl Bloch (1877)

Jesus covers a variety of subjects: lust, divorce, oaths, retaliation, giving to the needy, fasting, laying up treasure in Heaven, do not be anxious, judging others, ask and it will be given, the Golden Rule, a tree and its fruit, never knew you, build your house on rock, and…

"You have heard that it was said, 'You shall love your neighbor and hate your enemy.' But I say to you, Love your enemies and pray for those who persecute you, so that you may be sons of your Father who is in heaven. For He makes His sun rise on the evil and on the good, and sends rain on the just and on the unjust. For if you love those who love you, what reward do you have? Do not even the tax collectors do the same? And if you greet only your brothers what more are you doing than others? Do not even the Gentiles do the same? You therefore must be perfect, as your heavenly Father is perfect."

Perfect? Who can be perfect?

Consider His words carefully. He's speaking to those who are under the law. We are under grace, so some of His teaching may not be directly applicable. We are not able to achieve perfection, which is why we rely on Him.

Narrow Road
Matthew 7

Narrow Road of Virtue and Wide Road of Sin by Jan Micker (1599-1664)

He told them the way may be difficult.

"Enter by the narrow gate. For the gate is wide and the way is easy that leads to destruction, and those who enter by it are many. For the gate is narrow and the way is hard that leads to life, and those who find it are few.

The narrow gate is Christ. He said *I am the way and the truth and the life.* (John 14:6)

We are filled with His Spirit; thus, we *are being transformed into the same image from one degree of glory to another. For this comes from the Lord who is the Spirit.* (2 Corinthians 3)

Sermon Continues
Matthew 5-7

Sermon on the Mount by Ivan Makarov (1889)

And, of great importance is staying connected, the Lord's Prayer…

And when you pray, do not heap up empty phrases as the Gentiles do, for they think that they will be heard for their many words. Do not be like them, for your Father knows what you need before you ask Him. Pray then like this:

Our Father in heaven, hallowed be Your name. Your kingdom come, Your will be done, on earth as it is in heaven. Give us this day our daily bread, and forgive us our debts, as we also have forgiven our debtors. And lead us not into temptation, but deliver us from evil.

For if you forgive others their trespasses, your heavenly Father will also forgive you, but if you do not forgive others their trespasses, neither will your Father forgive your trespasses.

I am reminded of Psalm 100:4, which says *"Enter into His gates with thanksgiving, and into His courts with praise..."* What a good place to be!

His Authority
John 5

The Pharisees Question Jesus by James Tissot (1886-1894)

Jesus healed a paralytic on the Sabbath and then spoke to him in the temple.

The man went away and told the Jews that it was Jesus who had healed him. And this was why the Jews were persecuting Jesus, because He was doing these things on the Sabbath. But Jesus answered them, "My Father is working until now, and I am working."

This was why the Jews were seeking all the more to kill Him, because not only was He breaking the Sabbath, but He was even calling God His own Father, making Himself equal with God.

So, Jesus said to them, "Truly, truly, I say to you, the Son can do nothing of His own accord, but only what He sees the Father doing... For as the Father raises the dead and gives them life, so also the Son gives life to whom He will. For the Father judges no one, but has given all judgment to the Son, that all may honor the Son, just as they honor the Father. Whoever does not honor the Son does not honor the Father who sent Him. Truly, truly, I say to you, whoever hears My word and believes Him who sent Me has eternal life. He does not come into judgment, but has passed from death to life.

The Pharisees witnessed His miraculous works! They heard His stunning words! And yet failed to see the obvious and accept the truth!

Healing
Matthew 8

The Healing of Peter's Mother-in-law by James Tissot (1886-1894)

Here, Christ heals Peter's mother-in-law, who had a fever. Throughout His ministry, He healed many, including the blind, lame, crippled, paralyzed, deaf, dumb, lepers, and those with evil spirits or the demon-possessed.

What is the source of such power?

He even raised the dead, and for that the Pharisees decided He must die. (John 11:53)

Widow of Nain's Son
Luke 7

Jesus Resurrecting the Son of the Widow of Nain by Pierre Bouillon (1817)

First reported was the widow of Nain's son.

Soon afterward He went to a town called Nain, and His disciples and a great crowd went with Him. As He drew near to the gate of the town, behold, a man who had died was being carried out, the only son of his mother, and she was a widow, and a considerable crowd from the town was with her. And when the Lord saw her, He had compassion on her and said to her, "Do not weep." Then He came up and touched the bier, and the bearers stood still. And He said, "Young man, I say to you, arise." And the dead man sat up and began to speak, and Jesus gave him to his mother. Fear seized them all, and they glorified God, saying, "A great prophet has arisen among us!" and "God has visited his people!" And this report about Him spread through the whole of Judea and all the surrounding country.

Raising the Dead
Mark 5

The Daughter of Jairus by James Tissot (1886-1894)

Then a synagogue leader's child, Jarius' daughter.

While He was still speaking, there came from the ruler's house some who said, "Your daughter is dead. Why trouble the Teacher any further?" But overhearing what they said, Jesus said to the ruler of the synagogue, "Do not fear, only believe." And He allowed no one to follow Him except Peter and James and John the brother of James. They came to the house of the ruler of the synagogue, and Jesus saw a commotion, people weeping and wailing loudly. And when He had entered, He said to them, "Why are you making a commotion and weeping? The child is not dead but sleeping." And they laughed at Him. But He put them all outside and took the child's father and mother and those who were with Him and went in where the child was. Taking her by the hand He said to her, "Talitha cumi," which means, "Little girl, I say to you, arise." And immediately the girl got up and began walking (for she was twelve years of age), and they were immediately overcome with amazement. And He strictly charged them that no one should know this, and told them to give her something to eat.

Lazarus
John 11

Jesus Wakes Lazarus by Robert Wilhelm Ekman (1860)

And His friend Lazarus.

Jesus loved the family of Mary, Martha, and Lazarus, but when Mary sent word that her brother, Lazarus, was extremely ill, He delayed His coming to show His authority, and Lazarus died. He arrived four days later and wept.

Then Jesus, deeply moved, came to the tomb. It was a cave, and a stone lay against it. Jesus said, "Take away the stone." Martha, the sister of the dead man, said to Him, "Lord, by this time there will be an odor, for he has been dead four days." Jesus said to her, "Did I not tell you that if you believed you would see the glory of God?" So, they took away the stone. And Jesus lifted up His eyes and said, "Father, I thank You that You have heard Me. I knew that You always hear Me, but I said this on account of the people standing around, that they may believe that You sent Me." When He had said these things, He cried out with a loud voice, "Lazarus, come out." The man who had died came out, his hands and feet bound with linen strips, and his face wrapped with a cloth. Jesus said to them, "Unbind him, and let him go."

The Pharisees, hypocrites that they were, decided Jesus and Lazarus should both die. (John 12)

Power Flows
Mark 5/Matthew 9/Luke 8

Christ and the Woman with the Issue of Blood by Paolo Veronese (1565-1570)

Here we witness the power of faith. Belief in Him allowed the healing power to flow. This incident occurred while He was with Jarius.

And a great crowd followed Him and thronged about Him. And there was a woman who had had a discharge of blood for twelve years, and who had suffered much under many physicians, and had spent all that she had, and was no better but rather grew worse. She had heard the reports about Jesus and came up behind Him in the crowd and touched His garment. For she said, "If I touch even His garments, I will be made well." And immediately the flow of blood dried up, and she felt in her body that she was healed of her disease. And Jesus, perceiving in Himself that power had gone out from Him, immediately turned about in the crowd and said, "Who touched my garments?" And His disciples said to Him, "You see the crowd pressing around You, and yet You say, 'Who touched Me?'" And He looked around to see who had done it. But the woman, knowing what had happened to her, came in fear and trembling and fell down before Him and told Him the whole truth. And He said to her, "Daughter, your faith has made you well; go in peace, and be healed of your disease."

The power of God made this woman well.

Lord of the Sabbath
Matthew 12

Christ defends the plucking of the ears of grain on the Sabbath by Marten van Valckenborch (1580-1590)

Jesus went through the grainfields on the Sabbath. His disciples were hungry, and they began to pluck heads of grain and to eat. But when the Pharisees saw it, they said to Him, "Look, Your disciples are doing what is not lawful to do on the Sabbath." He said to them, "Have you not read what David did when he was hungry, and those who were with him: how he entered the house of God and ate the bread of the Presence, which it was not lawful for him to eat nor for those who were with him, but only for the priests? Or have you not read in the Law how on the Sabbath the priests in the Temple profane the Sabbath and are guiltless? I tell you, something greater than the Temple is here. And if you had known what this means, 'I desire mercy, and not sacrifice,' you would not have condemned the guiltless. For the Son of Man is Lord of the Sabbath."

Challenge of the Pharisees
Matthew 12

The Man with the Withered Hand by James Tissot (1886-1894)

He went on from there and entered their synagogue. And a man was there with a withered hand. And they asked Him, "Is it lawful to heal on the Sabbath?"—so that they might accuse Him. He said to them, "Which one of you who has a sheep, if it falls into a pit on the Sabbath, will not take hold of it and lift it out? Of how much more value is a man than a sheep! So, it is lawful to do good on the Sabbath." He healed him. *But the Pharisees went out and conspired against Him, how to destroy Him.*

Of course they challenged Him. They were committed to teaching the Law and did not realize He offered grace because He was the rest celebrated every Sabbath (Hebrews 4). We are now motivated by love not Law (1 Corinthians 16:14).

Doing Good
Luke 13

The Woman with an Infirmity of Eighteen Years by James Tissot (1884-1896)

He used such reasoning multiple times.

Now He was teaching in one of the synagogues on the Sabbath. And behold, there was a woman who had had a disabling spirit for eighteen years. She was bent over and could not fully straighten herself. When Jesus saw her, He called her over and said to her, "Woman, you are freed from your disability." And He laid His hands on her, and immediately she was made straight, and she glorified God. But the ruler of the synagogue, indignant because Jesus had healed on the Sabbath, said to the people, "There are six days in which work ought to be done. Come on those days and be healed, and not on the Sabbath day." Then the Lord answered him, "You hypocrites! Does not each of you on the Sabbath untie his ox or his donkey from the manger and lead it away to water it? And ought not this woman, a daughter of Abraham whom Satan bound for eighteen years, be loosed from this bond on the Sabbath day?" As He said these things, all His adversaries were put to shame, and all the people rejoiced at all the glorious things that were done by Him.

Woe to You
Matthew 12/23

Curses Against the Pharisees by James Tissot (1886-1894)

He called the leaders a brood of vipers because of their evil intent and warned them with seven woes.

Jesus rebuked evil but showed a compassionate love for those hurting and willing to listen.

Are we willing to listen?

Paul tells us *that for those who love God all things work together for good, for those who are called according to his purpose.* (Romans 8:28)

Hypocrisy
John 8

Jesus Christ and the Woman Taken in Adultery by Peter Paul Rubens (1614)

Of particular interest is the case of the woman taken in adultery.

The teachers of the law and the Pharisees brought in a woman caught in adultery. They made her stand before the group and *said to Jesus, "Teacher, this woman was caught in the act of adultery. The Law of Moses commanded us to stone such women. Now what do You say?" They were using this question as a trap in order to have a basis for accusing Him.*

But Jesus bent down and started to write on the ground with His finger. When they kept on questioning Him, He straightened up and said to them, "Let any one of you who is without sin be the first to throw a stone at her." Again, He stooped down and wrote on the ground.

At this, those who heard began to go away one at a time, the older ones first, until only Jesus was left, with the woman still standing there. Jesus straightened up and asked her, "Woman, where are they? Has no one condemned you?" "No one, Sir," she said. "Then neither do I condemn you," Jesus declared. "Go now and leave your life of sin."

Caught in the act? Where was her partner in this act? What bias and hypocrisy! Likely, Jesus wrote their names and sins on the ground. Jesus forgives all who come to Him!

Let us seek His mercy!

The Sower
Matthew 13 – Mark 4 - Luke 8

Jesus Preaches in a Ship by James Tissot (1886-1894)

He spoke to certain crowds in parables, probably because their hearts were not open.

One day, *Jesus went out of the house and sat beside the sea. And great crowds gathered about Him, so that He got into a boat and sat down... And He told them... "A sower went out... and as he sowed, some seeds fell along the path, and the birds came and devoured them. Other seeds fell on rocky ground, where they did not have much soil, and immediately they sprang up, since they had no depth of soil, but when the sun rose, they were scorched. And since they had no root, they withered away. Other seeds fell among thorns, and the thorns grew up and choked them. Other seeds fell on good soil and produced grain, some a hundredfold, some sixty, some thirty..."*

Then the disciples came and said to Him, "Why do You speak to them in parables?" Because they will hear and not understand He told them.

"Hear the parable: When anyone hears the word of the kingdom and does not understand it, the evil one comes and snatches away what has been sown in his heart. This is what was sown along the path. ...on rocky ground, this is the one who hears the word and immediately receives it with joy, yet he has no root in himself, but when tribulation or persecution arises on account of the word, immediately he falls away... thorns, this is the one who hears the word, but the cares of the world and the deceitfulness of riches choke the word, and it proves unfruitful... good soil, this is the one who hears the word and understands it. He indeed bears fruit and yields, a hundredfold, sixty, or thirty-fold."

Pearl of Great Price
Matthew 13

The Parable of the Merchant and the Pearl by Andrey Nikolaevich Mironov (2020)

Jesus explained some of the parables to the disciples, but these He did not explain. What do you think they mean?

The kingdom of heaven is like treasure hidden in a field, which a man found and covered up. Then, in his joy, he goes and sells all that he has and buys that field.

Again, the kingdom of heaven is like a merchant in search of fine pearls, who, on finding one pearl of great value, went and sold all that he had and bought it.

Most people imagine the treasure and pearl represent the kingdom of heaven. Probably not. What does God require for your salvation? Belief… nothing else.

Who paid everything? Christ, His divinity in heaven for a time, His liberty, His life. He is the man. He is the merchant, looking for great value.

You are that value! You are the treasure! You are the pearl of great price! He gave all. He suffered and died for your freedom!

Miracles
Matthew 14

Saint Peter Trying to Walk on Water by François Boucher (1766)

After one gathering where He taught, Jesus sent His disciples in a boat across the Sea of Galilee while He dismissed the crowd, then He climbed the mountainside to pray. Before dawn, He walked to them on the lake. They were struggling with strong winds and waves. They feared His appearance, but He set them at ease. Peter wanted to come to Him on the water. Jesus consented, but Peter's faith failed him, requiring Jesus to catch him. They made it to the boat and their destination, Gennesaret.

Jesus performed all kinds of miracles besides healing. He also calmed the storm (Mark 4). He dried up a fig tree (Mark 11). He directed a large catch of fish (Luke 5/John 21). He paid His taxes with a coin found in a fish (Matthew 17).

Who does such things? Certainly, nothing is too difficult for the Son of God and Son of Man.

We know why He came… to redeem mankind. But ponder His timing for a moment.

By using the life spans given in Scripture, some calculations estimate that Adam was created about 4000 B.C. Three seems to represent the Trinity. Four represents creation, the earthly realm, or the world, while five indicates grace or humanity. Six is the number of man, seven is perfection or completion, eight marks a new beginning, and there are others. You might find it useful or provocative to study what meaning numbers seem to have in Scripture.

Dealing with Demons
Mark 9/Luke 9/Matthew 17

The Possessed Boy at the Foot of Mount Tabor by James Tissot (1884-1896)

He handled demons…

One of the men in the crowd spoke up and said, "Teacher, I brought my son so You could heal him. He is possessed by an evil spirit that won't let him talk. And whenever this spirit seizes him, it throws him violently to the ground. Then he foams at the mouth and grinds his teeth and becomes rigid. So, I asked Your disciples to cast out the evil spirit, but they couldn't do it."

…when the evil spirit saw Jesus, it threw the child into a violent convulsion, and he fell to the ground, writhing and foaming at the mouth.

"How long has this been happening?" Jesus asked the boy's father. He replied, "Since he was a little boy. The spirit often throws him into the fire or into water, trying to kill him.

….He rebuked the evil spirit. "Listen, you spirit that makes this boy unable to hear and speak," He said. "I command you to come out of this child and never enter him again!" Then the spirit screamed and threw the boy into another violent convulsion and left him.

Afterward, when Jesus was alone in the house with His disciples, they asked Him, "Why couldn't we cast out that evil spirit?" Jesus replied, "This kind can be cast out only by prayer.

Control over Nature
Mark 4

Jesus Stilling the Tempest by James Tissot (1886-1894)

He could alter the environment with a word.

On that day, when evening had come, He said to His disciples, "Let us go across to the other side." And leaving the crowd, they took Him with them in the boat, just as He was. And other boats were with Him. And a great windstorm arose, and the waves were breaking into the boat, so that the boat was already filling. But He was in the stern, asleep on the cushion. And they woke Him and said to Him, "Teacher, do You not care that we are perishing?" And He awoke and rebuked the wind and said to the sea, "Peace! Be still!" And the wind ceased, and there was a great calm. He said to them, "Why are you so afraid? Have you still no faith?" And they were filled with great fear and said to one another, "Who then is this, that even the wind and the sea obey Him?"

We know who He is!

Transfiguration
Matthew 17-Mark 9-Luke9

The Transfiguration of Christ by Peter Paul Rubens (1605)

Jesus took with Him Peter and James and John, and led them up a high mountain by themselves. And He was transfigured before them, and His clothes became radiant, intensely white, as no one on earth could bleach them. And there appeared to them Elijah with Moses, and they were talking with Jesus. And Peter said to Jesus, "Rabbi, it is good that we are here. Let us make three tents, one for You and one for Moses and one for Elijah." For he did not know what to say, for they were terrified. And a cloud overshadowed them, and a voice came out of the cloud, "This is My beloved Son; listen to Him." And suddenly, looking around, they no longer saw anyone with them but Jesus only.

And as they were coming down the mountain, He charged them to tell no one what they had seen, until the Son of Man had risen from the dead. So, they kept the matter to themselves, questioning what this rising from the dead might mean.

Eyewitness testimony of Christ's divinity. Some believe Moses and Elijah will be the two witnesses of Revelation 11 because of their associated feats.

Let the Little Ones Come
Matthew 19

Jesus, Friend of the Little Ones by Vlaho Bukovac (1855-1922)

Jesus spent a great deal of time teaching throughout the land. In one place…*children were brought to Him that He might lay His hands on them and pray. The disciples rebuked the people, but Jesus said, "Let the little children come to Me and do not hinder them, for to such belongs the kingdom of heaven." And He laid His hands on them and went away.*

Jesus welcomes innocence and openness. He's loving and merciful. Willing, even eager, to forgive. Seek His grace!

I'm shocked anyone would be hostile to His message, to His sacrifice for our benefit. And then I reflect on the spiritual influences at work. We were warned about the forces of evil in the heavenly places (see Preface). I think it is more subtle and deceptive than we imagine. Resist and it will flee. (James 4:7)

Tribute Money
Matthew 22

The Tribute Money by Jacob Adriaensz Backer (1630s)

Jesus taught many lessons, but this one is a good summary.

The Pharisees, trying to entangle Jesus, asked Him if it was lawful to pay taxes to Caesar. Jesus' response is enlightening.

Jesus, aware of their malice, said, "Why put Me to the test, you hypocrites? Show Me the coin for the tax." And they brought Him a denarius. And Jesus said to them, "Whose likeness and inscription is this?" They said, "Caesar's." Then He said to them, "Therefore render to Caesar the things that are Caesar's, and to God the things that are God's." When they heard it, they marveled. And they left Him and went away.

And what, do you imagine, is God's?

Weeps over Jerusalem
Luke 19

He wept over Her by Enrique Simonet (1892)

And when He drew near and saw the city, He wept over it, saying, "Would that you, even you, had known on this day the things that make for peace! But now they are hidden from your eyes. For the days will come upon you, when your enemies will set up a barricade around you and surround you and hem you in on every side and tear you down to the ground, you and your children within you. And they will not leave one stone upon another in you, because you did not know the time of your visitation."

He knows the future and deeply cares. Jerusalem was destroyed in 70 A.D.

The Son likely mourns each and every person who fails to answer His call. Let it not be me.

Last Supper
John 13-17

Jesus Washing Peter's Feet by Ford Madox Brown (1852-1856)

They held a last supper shortly before His death.

It was just before the Passover Festival. Jesus knew that the hour had come for Him to leave this world and go to the Father. Having loved His own who were in the world, He loved them to the end.

The evening meal was in progress, and the devil had already prompted Judas, the son of Simon Iscariot, to betray Jesus. Jesus knew that the Father had put all things under His power, and that He had come from God and was returning to God; so, He got up from the meal, took off His outer clothing, and wrapped a towel around His waist. After that, He poured water into a basin and began to wash His disciples' feet, drying them with the towel that was wrapped around Him.

When He had finished washing their feet, He put on his clothes and returned to His place. "Do you understand what I have done for you?" He asked them. "You call Me 'Teacher' and 'Lord,' and rightly so, for that is what I am. Now that I, your Lord and Teacher, have washed your feet, you also should wash one another's feet.

The Son of God showed Himself a Servant to those He loves. He told them, *Greater love has no one than this: to lay down one's life for one's friends.*

And He loves you! How indeed do we respond?

Jesus' Prayer
John 17

The Last Supper in St. John's Church, Kolkata by Johann Zoffany (1787)

He ended the supper with a prayer… Oh, Father…

I have revealed You to those whom You gave Me out of the world. They were Yours; You gave them to Me, and they have obeyed Your word. Now they know that everything You have given Me comes from You. For I gave them the words You gave Me and they accepted them…

I am coming to You now, but I say these things while I am still in the world, so that they may have the full measure of My joy within them…

He prayed for us, too!

My prayer is not for them alone. I pray also for those who will believe in Me through their message, that all of them may be one, Father, just as You are in Me and I am in You. May they also be in Us so that the world may believe that You have sent Me. I have given them the glory that You gave Me, that they may be one as We are One— I in them and You in Me—so that they may be brought to complete unity. Then the world will know that You sent Me and have loved them even as You have loved Me…

Righteous Father, though the world does not know You, I know You, and they know that You have sent Me. I have made You known to them, and will continue to make You known in order that the love You have for Me may be in them and that I Myself may be in them…

Agony in Gethsemane
Mark 14

The Agony in the Garden of Gethsemane by Francesco Trevisani (1740)

They went to a place called Gethsemane, and Jesus said to His disciples, "Sit here while I pray." He took Peter, James, and John along with Him, and He began to be deeply distressed and troubled. "My soul is overwhelmed with sorrow to the point of death," He said to them. "Stay here and keep watch."

Going a little farther, He fell to the ground and prayed that, if possible, the hour might pass from Him. "Abba, Father," He said, "everything is possible for You. Take this cup from Me. Yet not what I will, but what You will."

Then He returned to His disciples and found them sleeping. "Simon," He said to Peter, "are you asleep? Couldn't you keep watch for one hour? Watch and pray so that you will not fall into temptation. The spirit is willing, but the flesh is weak."

Once more, He went away and prayed the same thing. When He came back, He again found them sleeping, because their eyes were heavy. They did not know what to say to Him.

Returning the third time, He said to them, "Are you still sleeping and resting? Enough! The hour has come. Look, the Son of Man is delivered into the hands of sinners. Rise! Let us go! Here comes My betrayer!"

And indeed, Judas Iscariot appeared towing soldiers to arrest Jesus, having received thirty pieces of silver for the act of identifying Christ.

The Sword
Matthew 10/Matthew 26

Taking of Christ by Gérard Douffet (1620)

Jesus knew His message of belief in Him would lead to strife.

Do not think that I have come to bring peace to the earth. I have not come to bring peace, but a sword. For I have come to set a man against his father, and a daughter against her mother, and a daughter-in-law against her mother-in-law. And a person's enemies will be those of his own household. Whoever loves father or mother more than Me is not worthy of Me, and whoever loves son or daughter more than Me is not worthy of Me. And whoever does not take his cross and follow Me is not worthy of Me. Whoever finds his life will lose it, and whoever loses his life for My sake will find it.

But He did not call for violence, for when one of His disciples used a sword at His arrest, He said:

Put your sword back into its place. For all who take the sword will perish by the sword. Do you think that I cannot appeal to My Father, and He will at once send Me more than twelve legions of angels? But how then should the Scriptures be fulfilled, that it must be so?

On Trial
John 18 - Mark 14-15

Jesus in the House of Annas by José de Madrazo y Agudo (1803)

Jesus faced four trials: in the house of Annas, before Caiaphas and the Sanhedrin, with King Herod, and before Pilate, the Roman Governor of Judea, since the Jews no longer had the authority to order capital punishment.

Judas returned the money he was given to betray Jesus and hanged himself. I imagine he never meant his betrayal to lead to death.

Jesus said very little. He knew how this was to end. It's why He came.

Annas berated Him and sent Him to the Sanhedrin.

Sanhedrin
Luke 22

Jesus appearing before Caiphus, Denial of Peter by Johann Georg Trautmann (1713-1769)

Peter was near one of the trials, and when questioned, he denied Jesus three times. He fled ashamed.

The council said, "If you are the Christ, tell us." But He said to them, "If I tell you, you will not believe, and if I ask you, you will not answer. But from now on the Son of Man shall be seated at the right hand of the power of God." So, they all said, "Are you the Son of God, then?" And He said to them, "You say that I am." Then they said, "What further testimony do we need? We have heard it ourselves from His own lips."

Then they took Him to Pilate to have Him killed.

King Herod
Luke 23

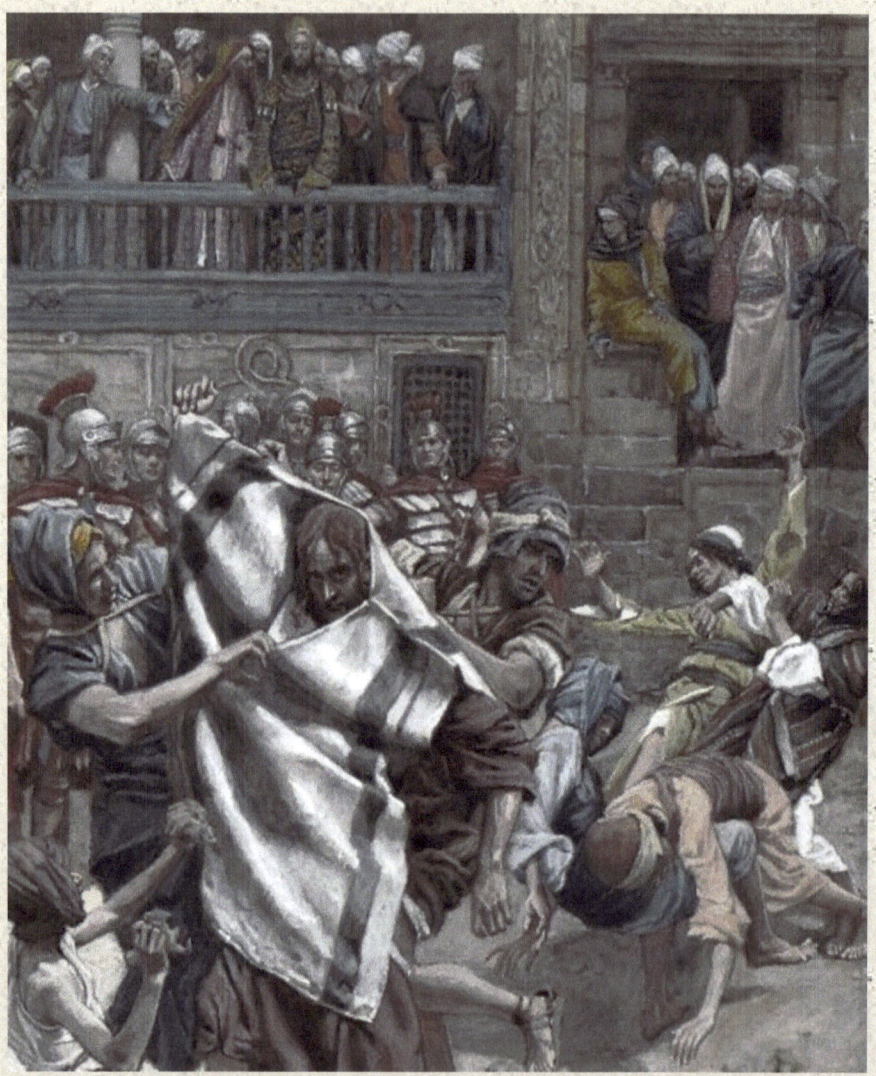

Jesus Before Herod by James Tissot (1886-1894)

When Pilate heard He was from Galilee, he sent Him to Herod.

Herod was very glad, for he had long desired to see Him, because he had heard about Him, and he was hoping to see some sign done by Him. So, he questioned Him at some length, but He made no answer. The chief priests and the scribes stood by, vehemently accusing Him. And Herod with his soldiers treated Him with contempt and mocked him. Then, arraying Him in splendid clothing, he sent Him back to Pilate.

Righteous Man
Matthew 27

The Message of Pilate's Wife by James Tissot (1886-1894)

When questioned by Pilate, Jesus offered no defense against the crime of sedition because He acknowledged He was King of the Jews, though He said His Kingdom was not of this world.

Curiously, Pilate's wife inserted herself during His trial.

Pilate was willing to release a prisoner due to the Passover and offered a choice between Jesus and a criminal named Barabbas.

For he knew that it was out of envy that they had delivered Him up. Besides, while he was sitting on the judgment seat, his wife sent word to him, "Have nothing to do with that righteous man, for I have suffered much because of Him today in a dream."

The crowd shouted to release Barabbas and crucify Jesus at the urging of the Pharisees.

Jesus was scourged and crucified.

Barabbas, by the way, is Aramaic and means Son of the Father!

Crucifixion
Matthew 27

Crucifixion of Christ by Paulo Gamba (1741)

And they crucified Him on Passover, this Lamb of God, who bore the sins of the whole world so that we might be set free.

Upon His death the environment was altered…

And behold, the curtain of the Temple was torn in two, from top to bottom. And the earth shook, and the rocks were split. The tombs also were opened. And many bodies of the saints who had fallen asleep were raised, and coming out of the tombs after His resurrection they went into the holy city and appeared to many. When the centurion and those who were with him, keeping watch over Jesus, saw the earthquake and what took place, they were filled with awe and said, "Truly this was the Son of God!"

God is Love
John 15/1 John 4

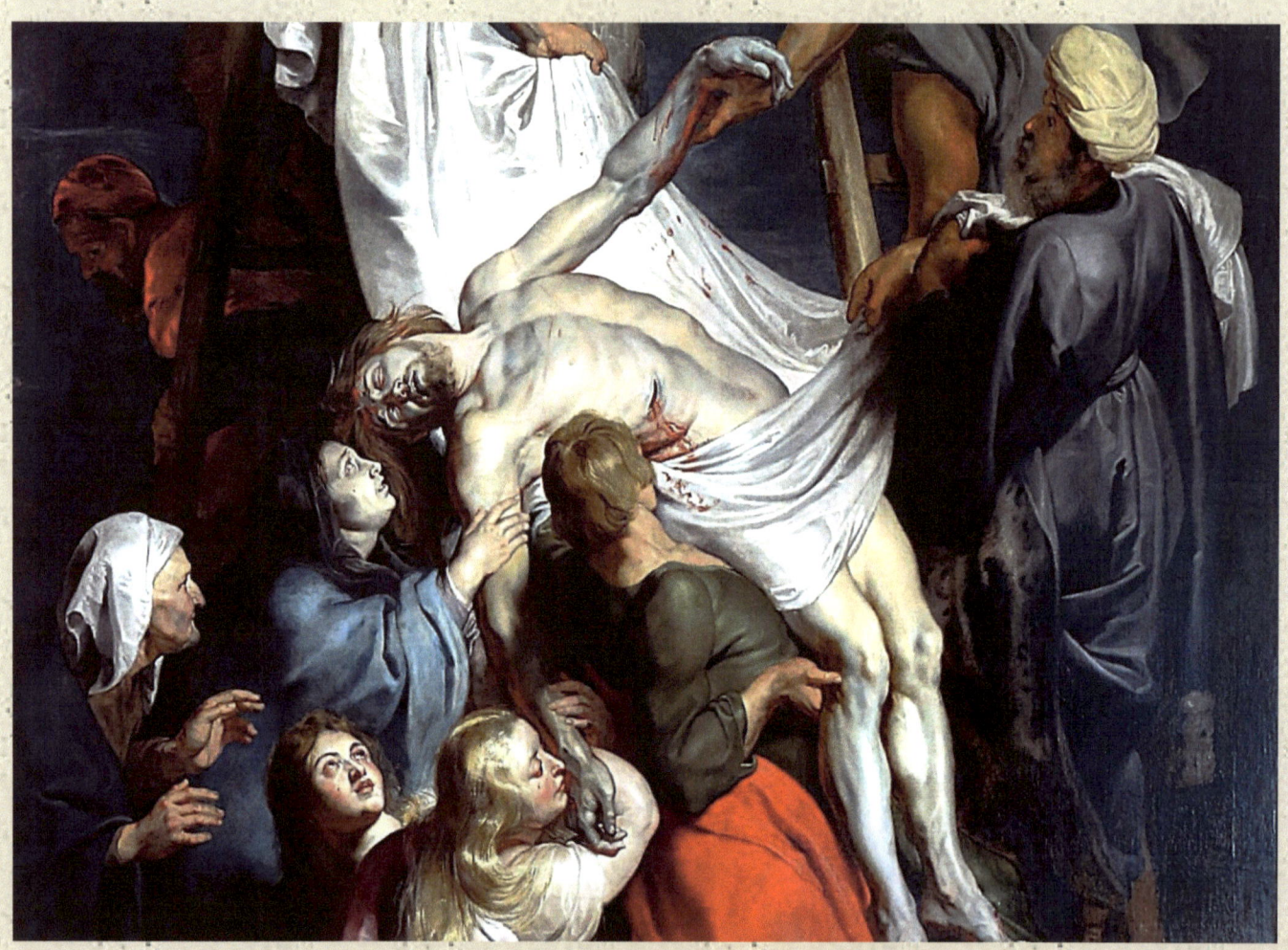

Descent from the Cross by Peter Paul Rubens (1617)

No greater love…

Sepulcher
Matthew 27

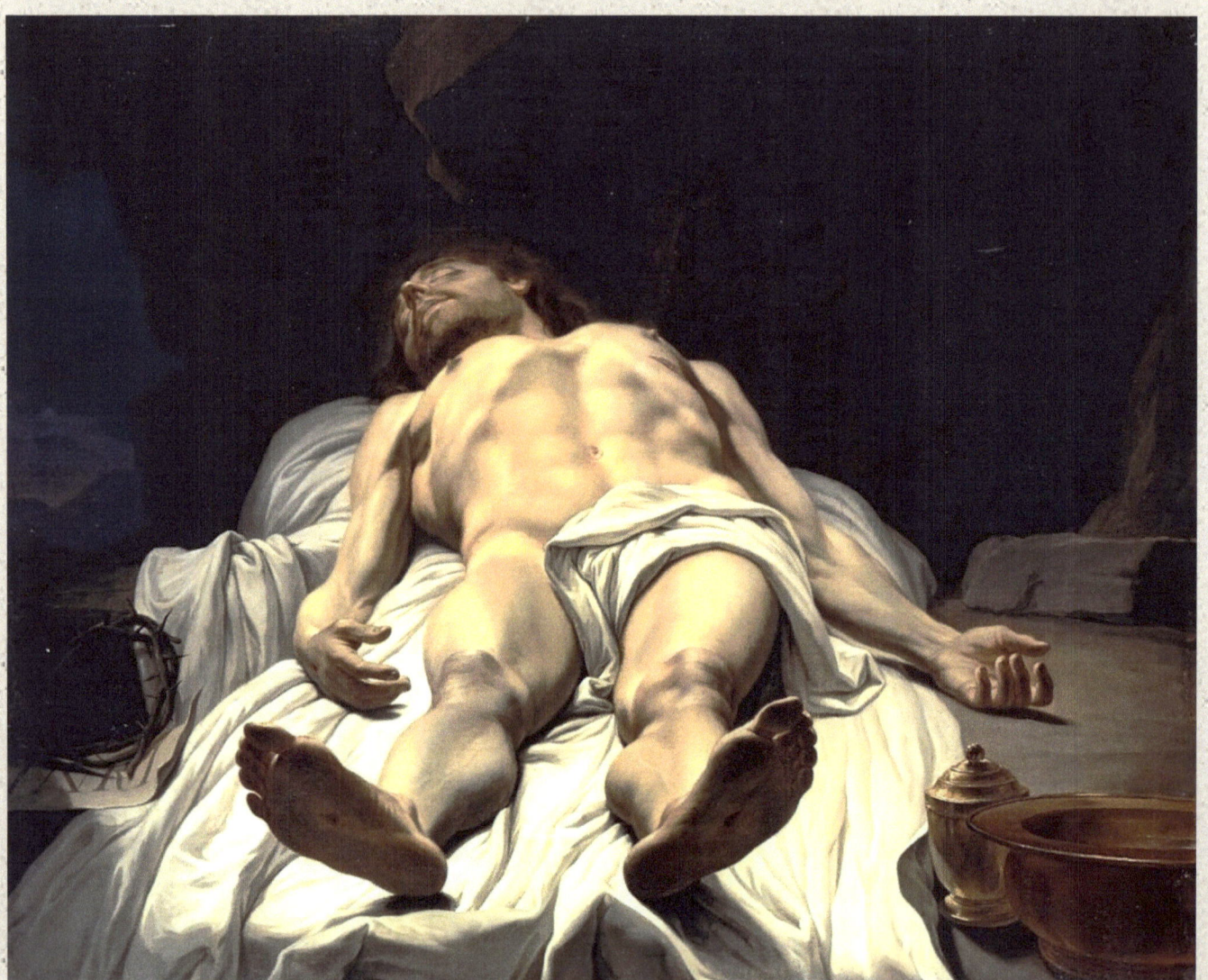

The Dead Christ by Johann Melchior Wyrsch (1779)

Then, before the Sabbath, they laid Him, this Son of God, in the tomb given by Joseph of Arimathea. This was on eve of the high day of Unleavened bread.

And while His body slept, His Spirit traveled to Sheol… this sinless Man who bore the sins of the world.

Sheol
1 Peter 3

The Vale of Tears Gustave Doré (1883)

For Christ also suffered once for sins, the righteous for the unrighteous, that He might bring us to God, being put to death in the flesh but made alive in the Spirit, in which He went and proclaimed to the spirits in prison, because they formerly did not obey, when God's patience waited in the days of Noah, while the ark was being prepared, in which a few, that is, eight persons, were brought safely through water.

I wonder what He saw, said, and heard while He spoke to those in prison. Then He returned.

Rising from the Dead
Matthew 28

Christ Resurrected by Peter Paul Rubens (1616)

And leaving the prisoners and the sins He bore, He rose three days later now bearing the *keys of Death and Hades*. (Revelation 1)

Proving, it would seem, He was the Son of God and seen by more than 500 people. (1 Corinthians 15)

And doing so on the prophetic feast of Firstfruits, established thousands of years earlier under Moses, and still celebrated by the Jews unknowingly today.

Enthusiasm
John 20

Saint Peter and Saint John Run to the Sepulcher by James Tissot (1886-1894)

Early on the first day of the week, Mary Magdalene discovers the stone has been rolled away from the tomb. She reports this to Peter and, we think, John, who race to verify its veracity. Peter trails the younger.

What enthusiasm in following Christ. They used this characteristic to proclaim and write about His life, message, and resurrection. Eyewitness testimony expressing the fact that the Son of God came to set us free from sin and death.

Examine Me
John 20

The Incredulity of Saint Thomas by Caravaggio (1601)

He showed Himself to His disciples, particularly "doubting Thomas," because he questioned the resurrection. Jesus encourages him to feel His wounds.

Now, the Lord Jesus Christ, Son of God and Son of Man offers us a choice - live one life or choose an eternal one. Follow Me, He says, and accept My gift.

Reconciliation
John 21

Feed My Sheep by Nicholas Poussin (before 1665)

Jesus came to the shoreline one morning while the disciples were fishing and assisted them in making a large catch, some of which they cooked. When they were done eating, Jesus asked Peter three times if he loved Him, and three times Peter's response was, "Yes." Each time Jesus tasked Peter to feed His sheep.

I raise this story to show that Jesus had forgiven Peter for denying Him, and that Peter felt remorse. But there is another hidden point to make. When Jesus said love the first two times, He used the Greek word *agape*, which is an all-encompassing, unconditional love. When He used the word a third time, He used the Greek word *philio*, which reflects friendship, even brotherly love. What reason would He have to do that?

Language makes a difference, which is why it's useful to have some reference that helps you appreciate the Greek, a very precise language. There are four commonly used Greek words for love. Besides the above, *storge* is family love, and *eros* is passionate love.

I use an interlinear bible which has the original word above the English.

Great Commission
Mark 16 – Acts 1

Ascension of Jesus Christ by Artus Wolffort (1617)

He was seen by many and gave a great commission to the apostles...

And He said to them, "Go into all the world and proclaim the gospel to the whole creation. Whoever believes and is baptized will be saved, but whoever does not believe will be condemned. And these signs will accompany those who believe: in My name they will cast out demons; they will speak in new tongues; they will pick up serpents with their hands; and if they drink any deadly poison, it will not hurt them; they will lay their hands on the sick, and they will recover."

So, then the Lord Jesus, after He had spoken to them, was taken up into heaven and sat down at the right hand of God. And they went out and preached everywhere, while the Lord worked with them and confirmed the message by accompanying signs.

Please note that Jesus gave this commission to the apostles, and the accompanying signs were designed to spread the Word with natural wonders. They apply to the apostolic age. We should not drink poison or grasp dangerous serpents to prove our faith today... remember His words to Satan in the wilderness, *You shall not put the Lord your God to the test.*

Consider who the speaker is addressing when deciding the applicability of an issue.

Pentecost
Acts 2

Pentecost by Juan Bautista Maíno (1615-1620)

When the day of Pentecost arrived, they were all together in one place. And suddenly there came from heaven a sound like a mighty rushing wind, and it filled the entire house where they were sitting. And divided tongues as of fire appeared to them and rested on each one of them. And they were all filled with the Holy Spirit and began to speak in other tongues as the Spirit gave them utterance.

This event, which marks the ability for all to receive the Holy Spirit, happened ten days after Christ's ascension. It occurred on the Feast of Weeks or Shavuot. Jesus said He had to leave in order to send the Spirit.

I tell you the truth: it is to your advantage that I go away, for if I do not go away, the Helper will not come to you. But if I go, I will send Him to you. And when He comes, He will convict the world concerning sin and righteousness and judgment: concerning sin, because they do not believe in Me; concerning righteousness, because I go to the Father, and you will see Me no longer; concerning judgment, because the ruler of this world is judged. (John 16)

Peter Preaching
Acts 2

St. Peter Preaching in Jerusalem by Charles Poërson (1642)

Peter was the apostle to the Jews. He healed a lame man and addressed the people.

"Men of Israel, why do you wonder at this, or why do you stare at us, as though by our own power or piety we have made him walk? The God of Abraham, the God of Isaac, and the God of Jacob, the God of our fathers, glorified His Servant Jesus, whom you delivered over and denied in the presence of Pilate, when he had decided to release Him. But you denied the Holy and Righteous One, and asked for a murderer to be granted to you, and you killed the Author of life, whom God raised from the dead. To this we are witnesses. And His name—by faith in His name—has made this man strong whom you see and know, and the faith that is through Jesus has given the man this perfect health in the presence of you all.

And now, brothers, I know that you acted in ignorance, as did also your rulers. But what God foretold by the mouth of all the prophets, that His Christ would suffer, He thus fulfilled. Repent therefore, and turn back, that your sins may be blotted out, that times of refreshing may come from the presence of the Lord, and that He may send the Christ appointed for you, Jesus, whom heaven must receive until the time for restoring all the things about which God spoke by the mouth of His holy prophets long ago. And all the prophets who have spoken, from Samuel and those who came after him, also proclaimed these days. God, having raised up His servant, sent Him to you first, to bless you by turning every one of you from your wickedness."

The Ethiopian
Acts 8

Saint Philip Christening the Ethiopian (17th century)
The painting was in the altar of the Saint Cornelius Chapel V, the chapel of the Triest family.

Acts 8 records a very unusual event.

Now an angel of the Lord said to Philip, "Go south to the road—the desert road—that goes down from Jerusalem to Gaza." So, he started out, and on his way, he met an Ethiopian eunuch, an important official in charge of all the treasury of the Kandake (which means "queen of the Ethiopians"). This man had gone to Jerusalem to worship, and on his way home was sitting in his chariot reading the Book of Isaiah the prophet. The Spirit told Philip, "Go to that chariot and stay near it."

The Ethiopian asked Philip to explain the text, which gave Philip the opportunity to tell him the good news about Jesus, after which the eunuch asked to be baptized.

When they came up out of the water, the Spirit of the Lord suddenly took Philip away, and the eunuch did not see him again, but went on his way rejoicing. Philip, however, appeared at Azotus and traveled about, preaching the gospel in all the towns until he reached Caesarea.

Miraculously transported to what is now known as Ashdod, miles away.

Some believe this event is linked to the Ark of the Covenant, which is today reportedly located in Aksum, Ethiopia, within the Church of Our Lady Mary of Zion.

Conversion of Saul
Acts 9

Conversion of Saul by Aelbert Cuyp (1645)

A young man named Saul was a devoted Jew who despised the growth of this Messiah sect, called the Way, and he did all he could to bring it to an end, arresting and imprisoning believers, thinking he was doing the work of God. He witnessed the stoning of the disciple Stephen, the first martyr.

He was later headed to the synagogues in Damascus to find members of the Way.

Now, as he went on his way, he approached Damascus, and suddenly a light from heaven shone around him. And falling to the ground, he heard a voice saying to him, "Saul, Saul, why are you persecuting Me?" And he said, "Who are You, Lord?" And He said, "I am Jesus, whom you are persecuting. But rise and enter the city, and you will be told what you are to do." The men who were traveling with him stood speechless, hearing the voice but seeing no one. Saul rose from the ground, and although his eyes were opened, he saw nothing. So, they led him by the hand and brought him into Damascus. And for three days he was without sight, and neither ate nor drank.

Filled with the Spirit
Acts 9

Ananias Restoring the Sight of St Paul by Jean II Restout (1719)

The Lord told a disciple named Ananias to visit Saul and lay hands on him to heal his blindness. He obeyed, and Saul was filled with the Holy Spirit.

Saul began to preach faith in Christ, for which others sought his life. At this time, he spent three years in Damascus and Arabia being instructed in the faith by the Lord (Galatians 1). Later, his name was changed to Paul.

Tabitha
Acts 9

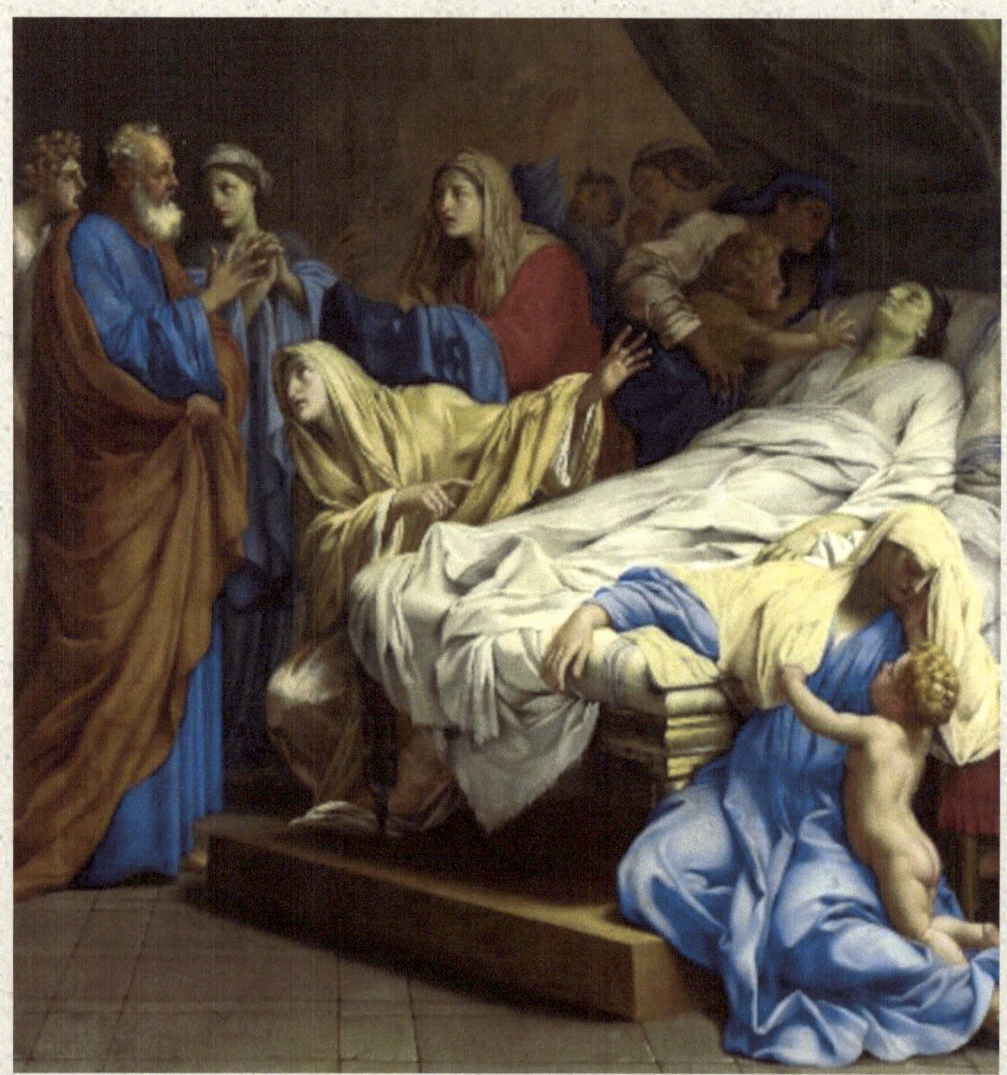

The Raising of Tabitha by Eustache Le Sueur: (1640-1645)

A disciple in Joppa named Tabitha (in Aramaic, Dorcas in Greek, both meaning gazelle) became ill and died. Other disciples heard Peter was close, so they sent for him. They told him of her charity and good works, and showed him the garments she made. He sent them out of the room and said:

Tabitha, arise. She did.

He presented her alive to the saints and widows. This became known throughout Joppa, and many believed in the Lord.

The Lord equipped His apostles with extraordinary power to spread knowledge of His divinity and sacrifice for the salvation of mankind.

Cornelius
Acts 10

Peter's Vision of a Sheet with Animals by Domenico Fetti (1619)

In a vision, an angel visited Cornelius, a centurion of the *Italian cohort, a devout man who feared God with all his household, gave alms generously, and prayed continuously to God*. Through a messenger, God told him to send for Peter, who was in Joppa. Meanwhile…

Peter fell into a trance and saw the heavens opened and something like a great sheet descending, being let down by its four corners upon the earth. In it were all kinds of animals, and reptiles, and birds of the air. And there came a voice to him: "Rise, Peter; kill and eat." But Peter said, "By no means, Lord; for I have never eaten anything that is common or unclean." And the voice came to him again a second time, "What God has made clean, do not call common." This happened three times, and the thing was taken up at once to heaven.

When the men from Cornelius arrived, Peter went with them to Caesarea, where Cornelius was expectantly waiting with his relatives and close friends. While they were talking…

…the Holy Spirit fell on all who heard the word… Then Peter declared, "Can anyone withhold water for baptizing these people, who have received the Holy Spirit just as we have?" And he commanded them to be baptized in the name of Jesus Christ. Then they asked him to remain for some days.

Thus, the Gentiles were welcomed into the family.

Disagreements
Galatians 2

The Separation of Saint Peter and Saint Paul by Giovanni Lanfranco (1671)

Many of the Jewish Christians continued to observe Jewish customs and tried to force them on the Gentiles, but Peter and I (Paul speaking) knew that was no longer necessary. This came to a head in Antioch.

When Cephas came to Antioch, I opposed him to his face, because he stood condemned. For before certain men came from James, he was eating with the Gentiles; but when they came, he drew back and separated himself, fearing the circumcision party. And the rest of the Jews acted hypocritically along with him, so that even Barnabas was led astray by their hypocrisy. But when I saw that their conduct was not in step with the truth of the gospel, I said to Cephas before them all, "If you, though a Jew, live like a Gentile and not like a Jew, how can you force the Gentiles to live like Jews?"

We ourselves are Jews by birth and not Gentile sinners; yet we know that a person is not justified by works of the law but through faith in Jesus Christ.

For through the law, I died to the law, so that I might live to God. I have been crucified with Christ. It is no longer I who live, but Christ who lives in me. And the life I now live in the flesh I live by faith in the Son of God, who loved me and gave Himself for me. I do not nullify the grace of God, for if righteousness were through the law, then Christ died for no purpose.

False Prophet
Acts 13

Saint Paul Blinds the False Prophet Barjésu by Nicolas-Pierre Loir (1650)

Barnabas and Saul were sent out by the Holy Spirit.

They went down to Seleucia, and from there they sailed to Cyprus. When they arrived at Salamis, they proclaimed the word of God in the synagogues of the Jews. And they had John to assist them. When they had gone through the whole island as far as Paphos, they came upon a certain magician, a Jewish false prophet named Bar-Jesus. He was with the proconsul, Sergius Paulus, a man of intelligence, who summoned Barnabas and Saul and sought to hear the word of God. But Elymas the magician (for that is the meaning of his name) opposed them, seeking to turn the proconsul away from the faith. But Saul, who was also called Paul, filled with the Holy Spirit, looked intently at him and said, "You son of the devil, you enemy of all righteousness, full of all deceit and villainy, will you not stop making crooked the straight paths of the Lord? And now, behold, the hand of the Lord is upon you, and you will be blind and unable to see the sun for a time." Immediately, mist and darkness fell upon him, and he went about seeking people to lead him by the hand. Then the proconsul believed, when he saw what had occurred, for he was astonished at the teaching of the Lord.

Athens
Acts 17

Sermon of St Paul Amidst the Ruins by Giovanni Paolo Pannini (1744)

Paul visited Athens and, standing at the Areopagus, said: *Men of Athens, I perceive that in every way you are very religious. For as I passed along and observed the objects of your worship, I found also an altar with this inscription: 'To the unknown god.' What, therefore, you worship as unknown, this I proclaim to you. The God who made the world and everything in it, being Lord of heaven and earth, does not live in temples made by man, nor is He served by human hands, as though He needed anything, since He Himself gives to all mankind life and breath and everything. And He made from one man every nation of mankind to live on all the face of the earth, having determined allotted periods and the boundaries of their dwelling place, that they should seek God, and perhaps feel their way toward Him and find Him. Yet He is actually not far from each one of us, for "In Him we live and move and have our being"; as even some of your own poets have said, "For we are indeed His offspring."*

Being then God's offspring, we ought not to think that the Divine Being is like gold or silver or stone, an image formed by the art and imagination of man. The times of ignorance God overlooked, but now He commands all people everywhere to repent, because He has fixed a day on which He will judge the world in righteousness by a Man whom He has appointed; and of this He has given assurance to all by raising Him from the dead.

Notice Paul didn't rant and rave about their false Roman gods. Rather, he spoke to the truth. They listened and wanted to engage again later. Some believed.

Eutychus
Acts 20

Saint Paul Resurrecting Eutychus by Jacques François Courtin (1672–1752)

Paul traveled a great deal. When he was in Troas, he gave a rather long speech until about midnight.

There were many lamps in the upper room where we were gathered. And a young man named Eutychus, sitting at the window, sank into a deep sleep as Paul talked still longer. And being overcome by sleep, he fell down from the third story and was taken up dead. But Paul went down and bent over him, and taking him in his arms, said, "Do not be alarmed, for his life is in him." And when Paul had gone up and had broken bread and eaten, he conversed with them a long while, until daybreak, and so departed. And they took the youth away alive, and were not a little comforted.

The Lord blessed Paul, who performed many miracles in order to bring others to faith.

And he gave them all the gospel… *For I delivered to you as of first importance what I also received: that Christ died for our sins in accordance with the Scriptures, that He was buried, that He was raised on the third day in accordance with the Scriptures…* (1 Corinthians 15)

Trial
Acts 20-26

Paul before King Agrippa and Governor Festus by Nikolai Bodarevsky (1875)

Paul faced trial before King Agrippa and Governor Felix for the trouble his presence stirred up in Jerusalem. Ostensibly, he went to carry alms to the poor believers, but also visited James and the elders, and went to the Temple, where attendees knew him and believed his teachings were against the Law, the Temple, and the people of Israel. He sparked a riot. Roman soldiers intervened, arresting Paul and preventing him from being harmed by the mob. He was later imprisoned in Caesarea for two years, awaiting trial.

Paul explained his whole story, almost bringing them to faith in Christ, but they were going to send him back for trial in Jerusalem, so he appealed to Caesar. They sent him to Rome.

Shipwreck
Acts 27

Landscape with the Shipwreck of Paul by Peter Paul Rubens (1625)

On their way to Rome, they were shipwrecked on the island of Malta.

Malta
Acts 28

Saint Paul Shipwrecked on Malta by Laurent de La Hyre (1630)

Luke narrating…

The native people showed us unusual kindness, for they kindled a fire and welcomed us all, because it had begun to rain and was cold. When Paul had gathered a bundle of sticks and put them on the fire, a viper came out because of the heat and fastened on his hand. When the native people saw the creature hanging from his hand, they said to one another, "No doubt this man is a murderer. Though he has escaped from the sea, Justice has not allowed him to live." He, however, shook off the creature into the fire and suffered no harm. They were waiting for him to swell up or suddenly fall down dead. But when they had waited a long time and saw no misfortune come to him, they changed their minds and said that he was a god.

Now, in the neighborhood of that place, were lands belonging to the chief man of the island, named Publius, who received us and entertained us hospitably for three days. It happened that the father of Publius lay sick with fever and dysentery. And Paul visited him and prayed, and putting his hands on him, healed him. And when this had taken place, the rest of the people on the island who had diseases also came and were cured. They also honored us greatly, and when we were about to sail, they put on board whatever we needed.

Paul was then off to Rome where he was imprisoned for two years. However, he continued to preach and write letters. He was eventually released.

Brother of Jesus
James

Saint James the Less by Peter Paul Rubens (1612-1613)

James is believed also to be known as James the Just, brother of Jesus, who wrote an epistle filled with wisdom. Let's set any identity controversy aside.

James begins by telling us to be joyful when our faith is tested and to ask God for wisdom, which He will gladly provide. He reminds us to be quick to hear, slow to speak, and slow to anger, because most anger is far from the righteousness of God and encourages us to be doers not just hearers of the word.

James emphasizes the need to bridle our tongue, which is the cause of much chaos, and to be impartial with others, not paying special deference to the wealthy. I think his saying "faith without works is dead" is sometimes misunderstood. We cannot earn our salvation. Rather, the indwelling Spirit molds our motivations and actions to be in sync with God.

We've already expressed this teaching, but it is worth repeating. *Wisdom from above is first pure, then peaceable, gentle, open to reason, full of mercy and good fruits, impartial and sincere.* Pay attention to the leading of the Spirit.

He warns us against worldliness and not to boast about the future, for we do not know what tomorrow will bring. He also warns that riches are temporary and can easily corrode. I imagine he read Matthew 6, which encourages us to *lay up treasures in heaven where neither moth nor rust destroys*. Finally, he encourages patience in suffering and expresses the value of prayer.

Thank you, James.

Another Brother
Jude

The Apostle Judas Thaddeus by Anthony van Dyck (1619-1621)

Again, there is debate regarding the identity of this Judas. So, let's just assume he is the brother of Christ and author of the epistle of Jude. He does begin by saying he is the brother of James.

Wanting to write about our common salvation, he rather found it necessary to warn us of the intent concerning denying or perverting the faith. He warns against those drawn to sensuality.

He recalls how Jesus saved a people out of Egypt but destroyed those who did not believe. He holds the angels who left their own position of authority in chains, but does not specify their action. Speculation is not useful, but he is condemning the pursuit of unnatural desires.

He lauds the Archangel Michael's response to the devil when contending over the body of Moses, indicating "the Lord rebuke you" was an elegant response. This is contrasted to speaking too many blasphemous things which the speaker does not understand.

Don't get worked up over things, be calm, keep the faith, pray in the Spirit, and patiently wait for the mercy of the Lord Jesus. Every circumstance has the Lord's watchful eye.

A wonderful message to believers about living with those driven by earthly passions. Do your best to help others.

Thank you, Jude.

Leader's Guidance
1 Peter and 2 Peter

Saint Peter by Pompeo Batoni (1740-1743)

Jesus gave Peter the keys to the kingdom (Matthew 16), making him the leader of the Church in Jerusalem. Peter wrote two epistles. They remind us of the temporary nature of this earthly life, the value of salvation through Christ, and the hope of life to follow.

The first epistle is written to the *elect exiles of the Dispersion*. Christians at this time were persecuted, even executed, and many fled to safer locations. Our faith will be tested, he said; be steadfast, be holy, be loving. Things of the flesh pass, but the Word of the Lord remains forever. Put away malice, deceit, hypocrisy, envy, and slander. Be good citizens, submit to authority, and respect and honor your spouse. *Finally, all of you have unity of mind, sympathy, brotherly love, a tender heart, and a humble mind. Do not repay evil for evil or reviling for reviling, but on the contrary, bless, for to this you were called, that you may obtain a blessing.*

His second epistle is to all believers and highlights the life to come as *partakers of the divine nature*. While some may claim this faith is a myth, he and many others were eyewitnesses to the Majestic Glory, the voice of God, and the miraculous events surrounding Christ. Beware of false prophets and teachers. They are headed to a very bad end, like the angels who sinned. The Lord is patient, not wishing any should perish, and read Paul's writings, which are Scripture.

Apostle to the Gentiles
Paul's Epistle to the Hebrews

Saint Paul by Pompeo Batoni (1740-1743)

Paul wrote the most content found in the New Testament. Thirteen epistles bear his name, but I'm convinced he wrote the book of Hebrews too. They all end with grace be with you, his signature ending. It is likely Paul avoided using his name in Hebrews because so many believed he abandoned the Law of Moses, not understanding his new insight from Christ. Paul loved the Old Covenant precepts, but he learned God's Age of Law was being replaced by God's Age of Grace, marked by the resurrection.

The Epistle to the Hebrews advises God's chosen to alter their view of the faith. It begins with… *Long ago, at many times and in many ways, God spoke to our fathers by the prophets, but in these last days He has spoken to us by His Son, whom He appointed the Heir of all things, through whom also He created the world. He is the radiance of the glory of God and the exact imprint of His nature, and He upholds the universe by the word of His power. After making purification for sins, He sat down at the right hand of the Majesty on high…*

Don't neglect your salvation, he pleads. Jesus is greater than Moses. Jesus is the great High Priest of the order of Melchizedek. The blood of Jesus paid the penalty for sin, which we all possess. You simply need faith. Turn to Him to be free.

Paul offered them freedom, but he knew their hearts were hardened… *to this day, whenever Moses is read, a veil lies over their hearts* (2 Corinthians 3). One day it will be removed.

Love (Agape)
1 Corinthians 13

Saint Paul Writing by Pier Francesco Sacchi (1520s)

We have two letters Paul wrote to the Corinthians, after he spent about 18 months with them on his second missionary journey. The most beautiful portion is chapter 13 in the first letter.

If I speak in the tongues of men and of angels, but have not love, I am a noisy gong or a clanging cymbal. And if I have prophetic powers, and understand all mysteries and all knowledge, and if I have all faith, so as to remove mountains, but have not love, I am nothing. If I give away all I have, and if I deliver up my body to be burned, but have not love, I gain nothing.

Love is patient and kind; love does not envy or boast; it is not arrogant or rude. It does not insist on its own way; it is not irritable or resentful; it does not rejoice at wrongdoing, but rejoices with the truth. Love bears all things, believes all things, hopes all things, endures all things.

Love never ends. As for prophecies, they will pass away; as for tongues, they will cease; as for knowledge, it will pass away. For we know in part and we prophesy in part, but when the perfect comes, the partial will pass away. When I was a child, I spoke like a child, I thought like a child, I reasoned like a child. When I became a man, I gave up childish ways. For now, we see in a mirror dimly, but then face to face. Now I know in part; then I shall know fully, even as I have been fully known.

So now faith, hope, and love abide, these three; but the greatest of these is love.

Doctrine
Romans

The Apostle Saint Paul by Anthony van Dyck (1618-1620)

Of all the epistles, Romans is the definitive tome on doctrine and the best read to understand God's intention in this Age of Grace. Excerpts…

The righteous shall live by faith.

His invisible attributes, namely, His eternal power and divine nature, have been clearly perceived, ever since the creation of the world, in the things that have been made.

Unbelievers *worship and serve the creature rather than the Creator.*

None is righteous, no, not one.

But now the righteousness of God has been manifested apart from the law, although the Law and the Prophets bear witness to it—the righteousness of God through faith in Jesus Christ for all who believe.

For sin will have no dominion over you, since you are not under law but under grace.

A wonderful epistle. Please read it for yourself.

Endtime Events
Thessalonians

Apostle Paul by Jan Lievens (1627)

1 and 2 Thessalonians are rather fascinating epistles. They discuss endtime events, which makes for an interesting read.

First - *The Lord Himself will descend from heaven with a cry of command, with the voice of an archangel, and with the sound of the trumpet of God. And the dead in Christ will rise first. Then we* (Paul is including himself) *who are alive, who are left, will be caught up* (Rapture) *together with them in the clouds to meet the Lord in the air, and so we will always be with the Lord.*

Second - *For the mystery of lawlessness is already at work. Only He who now restrains it* (Holy Spirit) *will do so until He is out of the way (Rapture). And then the lawless one* (Antichrist) *will be revealed, whom the Lord Jesus will kill with the breath of His mouth and bring to nothing by the appearance of His coming* (probably at the end of the Tribulation).

I inserted the common belief. We are anticipating the Rapture, but so was Paul. So, while trying to time this mystery is fascinating, don't get carried away. Stay in the Word. We ought to always be ready by living a life of faith. As Christ said in Luke 12, watch and be ready. May the grace of our Lord be with you.

Armor of God
Ephesians 6

The Emblem of Christ Appearing to Constantine by Peter Paul Rubens (1622)

The Christian life is a spiritual battle, as Paul explains in Ephesians. I imagine the Roman soldier guarding him inspired him with the metaphors he employs. We had best take his advice and be properly equipped.

Finally, be strong in the Lord and in the strength of His might. Put on the whole armor of God, that you may be able to stand against the schemes of the devil. For we do not wrestle against flesh and blood, but against the rulers, against the authorities, against the cosmic powers over this present darkness, against the spiritual forces of evil in the heavenly places. Therefore, take up the whole armor of God, that you may be able to withstand in the evil day, and having done all, to stand firm. Stand therefore, having fastened on the belt of truth, and having put on the breastplate of righteousness, and, as shoes for your feet, having put on the readiness given by the gospel of peace. In all circumstances, take up the shield of faith, with which you can extinguish all the flaming darts of the evil one; and take the helmet of salvation, and the sword of the Spirit, which is the word of God, praying at all times in the Spirit, with all prayer and supplication. To that end, keep alert with all perseverance, making supplication for all the saints, and also for me, that words may be given to me in opening my mouth boldly to proclaim the mystery of the gospel, for which I am an ambassador in chains, that I may declare it boldly, as I ought to speak.

Note: Constantine converted in 312 A.D. Evangelism is successful.

Spreading the Word
Epistles

Apostle Paul by Rembrandt (1657)

Paul wrote to the pastors and churches he had a hand in founding to encourage them to live a life of faithfulness.

He instructed the Galatians to live by grace, not the Law, and that they are free in Christ.

He encouraged the Philippians to maintain a Christlike attitude, and reminded the Colossians who they were in Christ.

He guides Timothy to godliness and sound teaching and charges him to carry on his gospel work.

He left Titus in Crete to set order in the churches there. Tough assignment. He advises him to rebuke insubordination and teach sound doctrine.

He addressed a letter to Philemon, Apphia, Archippus, and their house church, praising their faith and love for the Lord and requesting forgiveness and acceptance for their runaway slave, Onesimus, who came to faith.

Beloved Apostle
1 John, 2 John, 3 John

The Apostle Saint John the Evangelist by Peter Paul Rubens (1610-1612)

In his first epistle, John expresses his eyewitness testimony to the life and impact of Jesus Christ. He encourages us to walk in the light, extolls Christ as our advocate, and stresses that we do all things in love. He tells us not to love the world and to beware of antichrists, those who deny the Father/Son relationship, meaning the deity of Jesus Christ.

His second epistle was written to the elect lady and her children, meaning those who follow Christ. She is loved by him, in fact, all believers. Personally, I think he's writing to Mary, the mother of Jesus, who gave him responsibility for her upon His death. John emphasizes truth, love, and warning against deceivers.

In his last epistle, John writes to Gaius, a follower. Despite being a short, personal letter, he warns against Diotrephes and holds up Demetrius.

One book follows. John wrote Revelation.

Patmos
Revelation

Saint John the Evangelist on Patmos by Titian and Workshop (1640s)

Revelation describes the end of the age, the millennial reign of Christ on Earth, and the coming of the new Heaven and Earth. Much debate surrounds this text. What it means will become clearer as we get closer.

John talks to the glorified Lord Jesus Christ, who directs him to send letters to the seven churches. Some believe each church represents a period of church history. We are, some think, associated with the last church, Laodicea.

In chapter 4, John is called to heaven in the Spirit. Some believe this represents the rapture, since the church is no longer mentioned.

The scroll reveals end-time events, indicates the Tribulation is to last seven years, and its seals are opened one at a time by Christ. The first four seals release the four horsemen: conquest, war, famine, and death. The fifth seal shows the souls that were slain for the Word of God. Opening the sixth seal brings a great earthquake, chaos in the sky, and many seek to be hidden. Then 144,000 of Israel are to be sealed. Also, those whose lives were taken during the Great Tribulation are brought forward. Silence in heaven precedes the seventh seal, which gives us seven trumpets, which give us seven bowls. Then Jesus returns to Earth, rules for a thousand years with believers, Satan is defeated, and the new Heaven and Earth arrive.

Revelation is an interesting, action-packed read with loads of detail. Hope we don't experience much of it.

The Last Judgement
Revelation 20

Last Judgement by Michelangelo (1536-1541)

Christ will conduct a final judgment for those whose names are not found in the Book of Life. An unwelcomed end will result.

Your name is written in the book simply by acknowledging and accepting His sacrifice. Our Creator welcomes us.

I recall a night many years ago, standing below a smoking Mt. Etna. I was shaking my Bible in a clutching fist in the air, pleading to be sure of its truth, as I wanted to raise my three-year-old daughter correctly. A download must have occurred while sleeping because I rose the next morning and knew.

You can know too.

He wrote a book… one book… the greatest-selling and most widely disseminated book of all time. The Creator is quite capable of inspiring its writers and shepherding its truth over millennia. Read it and be open to its call.

And for those who imagine it's all good. Whatever you worship is fine. There are many ways to God. Don't be judgmental… let me remind you of Exodus 34:14: *for you shall worship no other god, for the Lord, whose name is Jealous, is a jealous God,* and John 14:6: Jesus is the way.

He is loving, patient and forgiving and now awaits the fulness of the gentiles (Hebrews 11). Accept Him or not. Your choice.

Dispensations
Bible

Ten Commandments by Anton Losenko (1737-1773)

Adam and Eve were innocent. They had but one commandment which they did not keep. After the fall, man lived listening to his own conscience. This only led to violence, resulting in the flood of Noah. God then allowed man to gather together, relying on their own government until Babel. Then we shifted to the Abrahamic Covenant and the family to keep order. Finally, God gave the Law to Moses from His own hands. However, violence and war persisted. Because of this, He sent His Son to die on a cross to relieve mankind of the task of attempting to earn their right to enter paradise. Humanity is simply incapable of this. We now live by His grace with His Spirit guiding us through love. We may want to do good, but the body we occupy will not easily yield. It is curious how most seem to want to return to living under the Law! Someday, the Son will return to reign for a thousand years, which will be more peaceful but still insufficient. A new Heaven and Earth are needed.

These are the dispensations of God, which reflect how He deals with man over time. We await the seventh dispensation, which is Christ's millennial reign. Seven seems to be the number of completion or perfection. Eight is the number of new beginnings.

The Aftermath

Christ with his Disciples by Andrey Nikolaevich Mironov (2016)

The New Testament reveals Jesus to be the Son of God, who accomplished His mission to reconcile His creation to Himself. More to follow.

Of His apostles, we believe all but John were martyred for their faith. They spread wide and far to preach the gospel. Peter traveled to Antioch and Rome. He was martyred. Paul extensively traveled throughout Anatolia (modern-day Turkey) and around the Aegean Sea, eventually reaching Rome. He was martyred. Thomas is believed to have traveled to India. He was martyred. Andrew traveled to Scythia and Greece. He was martyred in Patras. James the Greater is believed to have traveled to Spain. He and James the Less were martyred in Jerusalem. Matthew is supposed to have traveled to Parthia and Ethiopia. Martyred. Bartholomew went to Turkey and India. He was martyred. Philip labored in Scythia. Martyred. Jude traveled to the east of the Holy Land. Martyred. Simon the Zealot traveled to Egypt, Cyrene, Africa, and Britain. Martyred. Matthias replaced Judas Iscariot and is said to have traveled to Dacia and Britain. Martyred. John spent time in Ephesus and is believed to have been exiled to the island of Patmos. He died a natural death. Their remains can be found in churches in Europe and Asia today.

Who dies for their faith? I would imagine one who speaks what they believe to be truth.

Humble Beginnings

The Departure of the Apostles Going to Preach the Gospel by Robert Arsène (1870)

From such humble beginnings, the Way became the world's leading faith, based on eyewitness testimony of the Son of God's mission.

In 150 A.D., we estimate there were 40,000 believers. In 300 A.D., we estimate the number was 6-10 million. By 2000 A.D., the number increased to 2 billion.

The numbers now seem to be on a decline in the West. Do people care about the truth today? Share your faith. Share the Scripture.

Just Ask
Matthew 7/Luke 11/John 16

Saint Peter in Prayer Matthias Stom (1633-1640)

Not sure about things?

Ask, and it will be given to you; seek, and you will find; knock, and it will be opened to you. For everyone who asks receives, and the one who seeks finds, and to the one who knocks it will be opened. Or which one of you, if his son asks him for bread, will give him a stone? Or if he asks for a fish, will give him a serpent? If you then, who are evil, know how to give good gifts to your children, how much more will your Father who is in heaven give good things to those who ask Him!

Take your time. Clear your head. Resist distracting thoughts. Rest quietly and ask. The Lord will respond to your sincere queries. You were made in His image.

Witness
1 Peter 3/1 Corinthians 3

Saint John the Baptist Bearing Witness by Annibale Carracci (1600)

For those of us who have accepted Christ, what do we need to do?

Peter tells us…

In your hearts honor Christ, the Lord as holy, always being prepared to make a defense to anyone who asks you for a reason for the hope that is in you; yet do it with gentleness and respect…

And Paul revealed our works will be tested by fire. Do good.

Rejoice in Suffering
Romans 5

St Paul and Silas in Prison by Michael Václav Halbax (circa 1700)

We should even rejoice in suffering… *knowing that suffering produces endurance, and endurance produces character, and character produces hope, and hope does not put us to shame, because God's love has been poured into our hearts through the Holy Spirit who has been given to us.*

Peace and Security
1 Thessalonians 5

Allegory of Peace by Jean Baptiste de Champaigne (1668)

Now that we examined eyewitness testimony of Jesus Christ in the New Testament, clearly demonstrating His divine nature, what are we waiting and watching for?

Concerning the times and the seasons, brothers, you have no need to have anything written to you. For you yourselves are fully aware that the day of the Lord will come like a thief in the night. While people are saying, "There is peace and security," then sudden destruction will come upon them as labor pains come upon a pregnant woman, and they will not escape. But you are not in darkness, brothers, for that day to surprise you like a thief. For you are all children of light, children of the day. We are not of the night or of the darkness. So then let us not sleep, as others do, but let us keep awake and be sober.

When they say peace and security?

Have you heard these words recently?

Why?
Isaiah 46

God the Father by Jacob Herreyns I (18th century)

Why did He do it this way?

Remember He said, I am God, and there is no other; I am God, and there is none like Me, declaring the end from the beginning and from ancient times things not yet done.

So why do we have the fall, the struggle between good and evil? Why wait 4000 years to send His Son and a couple thousand years to chain evil, just to release him a thousand years later? Then starting anew?

We cannot be sure, but as believers, perhaps we have some insight…

My sense - the Father chooses those who accept His Son, which requires humbleness before God, acknowledgement of shortcomings, and a willingness to change. Evil filters those not suited for the coming task. Time provides space to gather the right number while demonstrating His requirements and love.

The Chosen
Matthew 22

Jesus Teaches the People by the Sea by James Tissot (1886-1894)

Many are called, but few are chosen.

Be among the chosen.

Illustrations and Art – From Wikimedia

Cover: The Risen Christ appearing to the Virgin by Jacques Stella (1640)
Christ and the Sinner by Andrey Mironov (2011)
God Creating by Jan Brueghel the Younger (17th century)
The Annunciation of the Virgin by Gregorio Martínez (1547-1598)
The Dream of Saint Joseph by Philippe de Champaigne (1642-1643)
Presentation of Jesus at the Temple by Jean André (1662-1753)
Saint Joseph and the Christ Child by Guido Reni (1640)
The Twelve-year-old Jesus in the Temple by Max Liebermann (1879)
The Youth of Our Lord by John Rogers Herbert (1847)
John the Baptist Baptizing Christ by Francesco Trevisani (1723)
Christ in the Wilderness by Ivan Kramskoy (1872)
Christ in the Wilderness by Moretto da Brescia (1515-1520)
The Calling of Saints Peter and Andrew by Caravaggio (1602–1604)
Marriage at Cana by Andrey Nikolaevich Mironov (2017)
Jesus Casting Out the Money Changers at the Temple by Carl Bloch (1800s)
Jesus Heals the Blind and Lame on the Mountain by James Tissot (1886-1894)
Christ and Nicodemus by Fritz von Uhde (1896)
Christ and the Samaritan Woman by Pierre Antoine Augustin Verlinde (1823)
Jesus Christ Teaching on Mountain by Sealino (2023)
The Sermon of the Beatitudes by James Tissot (1886-1896)
Sermon On the Mount by Carl Bloch (1877)
Narrow Road of Virtue and Wide Road of Sin by Jan Micker (1599-1664)
Sermon on the Mount by Ivan Makarov (1889)
The Pharisees Question Jesus by James Tissot (1886-1894)
The Healing of Peter's Mother-in-law by James Tissot (1886-1894)
Jesus Resurrecting the Son of the Widow of Nain by Pierre Bouillon (1817)

The Daughter of Jairus by James Tissot (1886-1894)
Jesus Wakes Lazarus by Robert Wilhelm Ekman (1860)
Christ and the Woman with the Issue of Blood by Paolo Veronese (1565-1570)
Christ defends the plucking of the ears of grain on the Sabbath by Marten van Valckenborch (1580-1590)
The Man with the Withered Hand by James Tissot (1886-1894)
The Woman with an Infirmity of Eighteen Years by James Tissot (1884-1896)
Curses Against the Pharisees by James Tissot (1886-1894)
Jesus Christ and the Woman Taken in Adultery by Peter Paul Rubens (1614)
Jesus Preaches in a Ship by James Tissot (1886-1894)
The Parable of the Merchant and the Pearl by Andrey Nikolaevich Mironov (2020)
Saint Peter Trying to Walk on Water by François Boucher (1766)
The Possessed Boy at the Foot of Mount Tabor by James Tissot (1884-1896)
Jesus Stilling the Tempest by James Tissot (1886-1894)
The Transfiguration of Christ by Peter Paul Rubens (1605)
Jesus Washing Peter's Feet by Ford Madox Brown (1852-1856)
Jesus, Friend of the Little Ones by Vlaho Bukovac (1855-1922)
The Tribute Money by Jacob Adriaensz Backer (1630s)
He wept over Her by Enrique Simonet (1892)
The Last Supper in St. John's Church, Kolkata by Johann Zoffany (1787)
The Agony in the Garden of Gethsemane by Francesco Trevisani (1740)
Taking of Christ by Gérard Douffet (1620)
Jesus in the House of Annas by José de Madrazo y Agudo (1803)
Jesus appearing before Caiphus, Denial of Peter by Johann Georg Trautmann (1713-1769)
Jesus Before Herod by James Tissot (1886-1894)
The Message of Pilate's Wife by James Tissot (1886-1894)
Crucifixion of Christ by Paulo Gamba (1741)

Descent from the Cross by Peter Paul Rubens (1617)
The Dead Christ by Johann Melchior Wyrsch (1779)
The Vale of Tears Gustave Doré (1883)
Christ Resurrected by Peter Paul Rubens (1616)
Saint Peter and Saint John Run to the Sepulcher by James Tissot (1886-1894)
The Incredulity of Saint Thomas by Caravaggio (1601)
Feed My Sheep by Nicholas Poussin (before 1665)
Ascension of Jesus Christ by Artus Wolffort (1617)
Pentecost by Juan Bautista Maíno (1615-1620)
St. Peter Preaching in Jerusalem by Charles Poërson (1642)
Saint Philip Christening the Ethiopian (17th century). The painting was in the altar of the Saint Cornelius Chapel V, the chapel of the Triest family.
Conversion of Saul by Aelbert Cuyp (1645)
Ananias Restoring the Sight of St Paul by Jean II Restout (1719)
The Raising of Tabitha by Eustache Le Sueur: (1640-1645)
Peter's Vision of a Sheet with Animals by Domenico Fetti (1619)
The Separation of Saint Peter and Saint Paul by Giovanni Lanfranco (1671)
Saint Paul Blinds the False Prophet Barjésu by Nicolas-Pierre Loir (1650)
Sermon of St Paul Amidst the Ruins by Giovanni Paolo Pannini (1744)
Saint Paul Resurrecting Eutychus by Jacques François Courtin (1672–1752)
Paul before King Agrippa and Governor Festus by Nikolai Bodarevsky (1875)
Landscape with the Shipwreck of Paul by Peter Paul Rubens (1625)
Saint Paul Shipwrecked on Malta by Laurent de La Hyre (1630)
Saint James the Less by Peter Paul Rubens (1612-1613)
The Apostle Judas Thaddeus by Anthony van Dyck (1619-1621)
Saint Peter by Pompeo Batoni (1740-1743)
Saint Paul by Pompeo Batoni (1740-1743)
Saint Paul Writing by Pier Francesco Sacchi (1520s)

The Apostle Saint Paul by Anthony van Dyck (1618-1620)
Apostle Paul by Jan Lievens (1627)
The Emblem of Christ Appearing to Constantine by Peter Paul Rubens (1622)
Apostle Paul by Rembrandt (1657)
The Apostle Saint John the Evangelist by Peter Paul Rubens (1610-1612)
Saint John the Evangelist on Patmos by Titian and Workshop (1640s)
Last Judgement by Michelangelo (1536-1541)
Ten Commandments by Anton.Losenko (1737-1773)
Christ with his Disciples by Andrey Nikolaevich Mironov (2016)
The Departure of the Apostles Going to Preach the Gospel by Robert Arsène (1870)
Saint Peter in Prayer Matthias Stom (1633-1640)
Saint John the Baptist Bearing Witness by Annibale Carracci (1600)
St Paul and Silas in Prison by Michael Václav Halbax (circa 1700)
Allegory of Peace by Jean Baptiste de Champaigne (1668)
God the Father by Jacob Herreyns I (18th century)
Jesus Teaches the People by the Sea by James Tissot (1886-1894)
The Risen Christ appearing to the Virgin by Jacques Stella (1640)

Author

Commander George J Thielemann (USN, Ret) and his wife Telli

BA Psychology University of Wisconsin (Madison), MAT Education Northwestern University, MA National Security Naval War College, USN service 1976-2005, including Naval Flight Officer hunting Russian submarines from P3C aircraft, ASWOC Director Keflavik Iceland, Officer Candidate School Director, USAF Academy Assistant Professor of Political Science, CCG-7 N6 overseeing afloat Naval Force communications in the Arabian Sea for Afghan Operation Enduring Freedom after 9/11. Elementary School Teacher 1973-1976 and 2005-2019, Peace Corps Thailand volunteer until Covid shutdown worldwide 2020. Lifelong Biblical scholar. Both George and Telli are cancer survivors, and volunteer for various organizations, including Hospice.

Editor

Pastor Charlie Garrett and his wife Hideko

Charlie attended Southern Evangelical Seminary and Bible College and graduated Magna Cum Laude in 2009. He was ordained at Grace Baptist Church, Sarasota in 2010. He is the pastor of the Superior Word Church. His teachings air online. He has written an analysis of every verse in the Bible from Romans 1:1 to Revelation 22:11. His sermons include detailed studies in Hebrew and Greek as well as the cultural, historical, and pictorial aspects of the text presented. Charlie has been married to his wife, Hideko, for 41 years. They have two grown children and a house full of Chihuahuas.

The Volume of the Book
Matthew – Revelation

The Risen Christ appearing to the Virgin by Jacques Stella (1640)

Reviewed by Carol Thompson for Readers' Favorite
Review Rating: 5 Stars
7 July, 2025

Volume of the Book: Christ in the New Testament is a deeply insightful exploration of the life and mission of Jesus Christ as revealed in the New Testament. The book serves as a companion to its predecessor, Volume of the Book: Christ in the Old Testament, and focuses on how prophecy was fulfilled through Christ's love, sacrifice, and teachings. It is a comprehensive study that blends scriptural analysis, historical context, and theological reflection. The book is structured to guide readers through key events in the New Testament, from the birth of Jesus to His resurrection and ascension. Each chapter is enriched with vivid descriptions, scriptural references, and artistic illustrations that bring the biblical narrative to life. The inclusion of artwork, ranging from classical masterpieces to modern interpretations, adds a visual dimension that enhances the text.

The author's writing is scholarly, and he makes complex theological concepts understandable for readers of varying levels of biblical knowledge. His background as a lifelong biblical scholar and his personal experiences as a cancer survivor add depth to his reflections. The book also benefits from the editorial expertise of Pastor Charlie Garrett, whose detailed studies in Hebrew and Greek ensure the theological soundness of the work. The author emphasizes the humanity and divinity of Christ, as well as the transformative power of His teachings. It encourages readers to reflect on their own faith journey and challenges them to live a life of devotion and service. Volume of the Book is a beautifully written resource for anyone seeking to deepen their understanding of the New Testament and the life of Jesus Christ.

www.ingramcontent.com/pod-product-compliance
Lightning Source LLC
Chambersburg PA
CBHW040722060526
44119CB00080B/296